SAN FRANCISCO THEATER:

COMPANY
—— OF THE ——
GOLDEN HIND

—— BY ——
RACHMAEL BEN-AVRAM

Dedicated to the Memory of
Hallie Flanagan
and to
Suzanna Hart, Mary Burke Morris
Gerard Lespinette

Also by Rachmael Ben-Avram
THE ACT AND THE IMAGE

TABLE OF CONTENTS

1 - GRASS ROOTS FEVER

The Company of the Golden Hind was my dream of a theater, and the dream took shape as my life took shape. This is my story of the Company of the Golden Hind, a theater which I brought to life in San Francisco in 1951. The Company of the Golden Hind was one of the many grass roots theater companies across the country that were springing up after World War II. The Federal Theater, created in 1935, was for so many theater minded people like myself, the most electrifying inspiration of our lives. The history of the Federal Theater proves it to have been the most significant theater event in the history of our country. To understand better how the Golden Hind, so typical of the multitude of mid to late twentieth century regional theaters in America, came to be, we need to look back to the 30's.

By the end of the century, several hundred regional theaters had emerged from the creative soil prepared in the 1930's by the Federal Theater Project, a division of the Federal Works Progress Administration, known as the WPA. In our cities of today, large and small,- Akron and Albany, Hartford and Houston, Charlotte and Chicago,

Dallas and Des Moines, Minneapolis and Milwaukee, Seattle and San Francisco, Washington, D.C. ... the list goes on ... we now see a host of regional theaters that have taken up residence in these communities, supported by public and private funds, by regular and faithful subscription audiences, and functioning through the coordinated efforts of professionally trained and experienced actors, directors, designers, as well as technical and business staffs. These regional companies, with their mix of professional (meaning trained and paid), as well as volunteer staffs, meet their payrolls regularly, and all maintain their valued and respected popularity in their communities, some even winning national recognition..

To my mind, The Company of the Golden Hind would have been an unrealized dream had there not been a Federal Theater whose founding director was an extraordinary woman named Hallie Flanagan.

To understand better the importance of the Federal Theater Project, and its influence on the emergence of our own national theater, we need to recall the origins and development of theater in these United States. In the colonies, and even after the establishment of the republic, the American theater consisted almost entirely of imported companies from England. During the eighteenth and nineteenth centuries, American theater continued to be almost exclusively British in origin. British actors arrived on our shores and performed principally in Philadelphia and New York. The rest of the country made do with occasional touring productions of the best shows originating in these two cities. The notable exception was San Francisco, way out West, where San Franciscans enjoyed a rich culture soon after the Gold Rush. The histories of the Gold Coast, as it came to be called, describe many flourishing theaters in San Francisco, including a music hall and an opera house of huge proportions, unique among most other cities across the country.

During the first few decades of the twentieth century, Broadway became the theatrical center of the country, with every production a commercial venture designed to bring profits to its investors. Producers on Broadway were essentially entrepreneurs under the spell of the theater.

Some producers also ruled the stage as the company's director and star actor. Most utilized their own money with additional funds from adventurous theater buff investors. A few repertory companies in major cities did start up in the late 18th century (Ford's Theater in Washington, where Lincoln was murdered, comes to mind).

The Broadway theater, however, was entirely a commercial operation in New York City, and the rest of the country had to be satisfied with touring productions with Broadway stars performing one or more weeks at each stop-over city stretching from New York to San Francisco. There were some touring companies, such as those offering the Shakespearean repertoire, which continued to cover the continent until the 1940's. But these soon disappeared as World War II started.

In 1935, thanks to the imagination and determination of President Roosevelt and Harry Hopkins and Hallie Flanagan, the two individuals to whom he delegated the task, the country saw the creation of our first national theater. Its brief but very significant story is given a full account by its creator and director, Hallie Flanagan, herself, in her fascinating and spine-tingling account, published under the title "Arena".

The Federal Theater Project, as it was called, was created as part of the Works Progress Administration, or WPA, a program which President Franklin Delano Roosevelt, soon after his election in 1932, conceived to meet the challenge of the Great Depression. It was a keystone of his strategy for dealing especially with the massive unemployment holding the entire country in its grip. Theater, as an industry, was added on, in 1935, to the trades and other industries covered by the WPA. It brought living theater performances to all the cities cited above. The main purpose of the Federal Theater was to put theater people to work. It was responsible for employing thousands of unemployed people who, as professionals, earned their livelihood in the theater. That meant not only actors and directors, but scene designers and painters, costumers and musicians, box-office people, set builders, lighting technicians, and any other theater workers necessary to any stage production. The project had, in addition, an equally important objective: to develop a people's theater with a nationwide audience composed of a public drawn from all social and economic levels of American society.

All told, there were approximately 30,000 men and women employed nationwide by the Federal Theater once it got going. And it came into being because of the extraordinary vision, energy, and commitment of Hallie Flanagan, that one person in America who accepted the task of creating and directing the first and only federally financed theater in our country's history.

Neither Flanagan's name nor her work have received the honor they deserve. Hers is a name almost totally unfamiliar to the millions of today's theater-goers in our country. She is unknown even to most theater people now working in those regional theaters across America where the joint visions of FDR and Flanagan planted the seeds that we see in full flower today.

By 1935, the WPA had already provided millions of jobs for unemployed construction crews and highway builders, musicians and artists, farm workers and ditch diggers. It was that year that FDR asked his right hand man, Harry Hopkins, to do something about the unemployed workers from the theater. Hopkins called on Hallie Flanagan, who had been, some years before, a classmate with him at Grinnell College in Iowa. She had studied theater and playwriting with the renowned Professor Baker at Harvard, then gone on to join the faculty at Vassar where she created a theater department and the Vassar Experimental Theater that brought her national attention. Hopkins called on her to come to Washington to talk about creating a Federal Theater which FDR wanted to see in operation in every state of the union. In addition to Flanagan, Hopkins also appealed to some of Broadway's brightest theater people. None of them saw any possibility of succeeding with such a daunting challenge. Even Flanagan herself turned him down at first. She told him that the project would have a better chance of success if he could recruit a well known Broadway professional rather than a university theater person like herself. He didn't agree. He persevered, and persuaded her to accept the challenge. It turned out he was right.

Hallie Flanaan not only created the Federal Theater; she also awakened in the country an audience for living theater. In astonishing numbers, the audiences came to see their local theater companies, even as the film industry was growing to its eventual gargantuan proportions.

As Director of the Federal Theater, Hallie Flanagan was called on to promote the project in magazines, to do interviews with journalists, and to make speeches in all the cities and towns reached by the Project. Her high spirits, her unwavering dedication, and her infectious enthusiasm knew no bounds. I should know; I was one of the infected.

She was the first to speak of a "grass roots theater" when she made presentations of her plans for the Federal Theater in the cities and towns where she looked for community support. Under the project's charter, the Federal government paid all salaries, while the other costs, including rent, electricity, heating, scenery, costumes, and advertising, were paid for by the community. She made the heartland of America the heartland of the American theater. We now take for granted our flourishing regional theater, but it didn't exist until Hallie Flanagan introduced living theater in every state of the union, even where no theater had ever been seen before.

From its inception, there were attacks from the hard right-wing conservatives in the Congress. The Federal Theater was accused of being a Communist plot. The plays, some of which shed light on uncomfortable inequalities in American society, were accused of being left-wing propaganda. Roosevelt was accused of creating a popular theater to transform America into a Socialist state. Support for the Federal Theater Project came quickly from the political left and from the mainstream stars and underlings in the Broadway professional theater. To no avail. The Federal Theater Project had its funds cut off by Congress during 1939, its fourth season. Its passing was mourned all over the country, from New York to California. It wasn't until after World War II that the seeds planted by Flanagan began to sprout all over the country in the same cities to which Flanagan had first brought living theater.

Sometime around 1950, once the country began to experience its recovery from World War II, cities which previously would see an occasional Broadway production on tour with a featured Broadway star, started to develop and support their own resident companies. Sometimes these were university theater groups; sometimes they were amateur community groups which evolved into partially and then fully professional companies. In a national census of operating theaters, taken in 2006 by the Theater Communications Group, a network of regional theaters across the nation, the record showed more than 477 regional theaters, operating from coast to coast, their roots in the Federal Theater of the 30's (It's surprising so many of these same companies are now totally unaware of their debt owed to Hallie Flanagan, and are even ignorant of her name.)

This, then, is the story of a single seed planted by Flanagan's Federal Theater Project that took root and blossomed years later in Northern California. I speak of

The Company of the Golden Hind, which flourished in San Francisco and Berkeley for ten years, from 1951-1961. Together with my wife, Suzanna Hart, we created the company, and what follows is a personal account of what we did and how we lived it, what were our inspirations, our aspirations, and our achievements.

I have never had the habit of keeping a diary, so whatever I record here I pull up out of my store of memories. Some dates may be off a bit, but the events are true and close to being accurately dated. My very first experience of the theater was when I was four years old, and my immigrant Jewish mother took me with her to the Second Avenue Yiddish Theater on New York's Lower East Side where we saw Maurice Schwartz in a melodrama. I remember sitting in a box, on Mama's knee, and seeing this old man in a long black beard and long black coat being dragged onto the stage, tied up, with a mob ready to lynch him. I shrieked with empathetic fear, and started to cry with such vigor that Mama had to carry me into the lobby where we waited until the end of the show before taking the subway home to the Bronx. Evidently I had the same reaction to the circus. Mama reminded me years later, that when we went to my first, and last, circus at Madison Square Garden, I cried to see the clowns beating up on each other, even though it made everyone else in the audience laugh with delight. So, no more circuses for me.

My next theatrical experience, which remains so vivid in my memory, took place in the summer of 1937. I was twelve and the Children's Theater of the Federal Theater Project performed "The Emperor's New Clothes" out-of-doors in the Bronx on the street in front of an apartment house where a playmate of mine lived. I can still see the huge trailer truck parked crosswise at the end of the block with the whole side of the truck dropped down to the street level. We saw an entire theater stage on the truck-bed, with its own scenery and lights. The costumes the actors wore reminded me of illustrations from my favorite fairy tale books. As the lights came up, three of the actors jumped down from the stage and played catch with a large bean bag they threw back and forth above our heads as we sat in the street. It was a balmy summer's night. Once in a while one of us in the audience would catch the bean bag as it sailed above our heads and, with daring and delight, throw it back to them. The actors made some jokes to make us laugh. After maybe ten minutes or so, they jumped up onto the stage and the play began. I was transported to a veritable Wonderland.

After the show I told my chum I could hardly wait to see another show. I asked him to look into it, but we could never find out when the truck and the actors would be coming back. It was as if I had found my first love, only to have it too quickly disappear. I still sometimes feel a longing for that enchantment which first possessed me when I was in the throes of that experience of children's theater.

A year or so year later, I was a student at Townsend Harris High, and I acted in the annual school play staged by one of our English teachers, Lester Winter. It was Lester who became one of my mentors in the years that followed, through City College and then the University of California. At Townsend Harris, it was my first time on a stage and I clearly recall the play, an English farce called "The Man in the Bowler Hat". Townsend Harris was an all boys school and I, in drag, played the Leading Lady. Following our two performances of "The Man in the Bowler Hat," our teacher, Lester, took us all to Broadway to see the visiting Abbey Theater in Sean O'Casey's "Juno and the Paycock". I recall we each paid our 55 cents for the least expensive seats, and filled most of the last row of the balcony at the Ambassadors Theater on Broadway. How extraordinarily fortunate I was to have the Abbey's production of this O'Casey classic as my first exposure to living Broadway theater. Even without a diary to jog my memory, I can easily see before me that last row of seats as we filed in. The actors, stage, and sets are still vividly alive in front of me. Sara Algood and Barry Fitzgerald played the desperate and endearing couple, Juno and her "Paycock," with Arthur Shields as Joxer. I left the theater with the sound of their Irish brogue making music in my head. By the time the evening was over, I could feel the theater coursing in my blood. I was hooked.

Two years later, I was a student at New York's City College, and by that time I had become addicted to my fifty-five cent seats in the last rows of Broadway theaters. I found Hallie Flanagan's **Arena** in the college library, laying out the whole story of the recently closed Federal Theater Project. I also read **Dynamo**, Flanagan's account of her earlier experimental theater at Vassar. Almost like an addiction, my dream took hold in my consciousness. I was determined to carry on Flanagan's mission and pay her the homage due her for her vision of a grass roots theater, as she described it in the closing words of her book, **Arena:**

> The President of the United States in writing to me of his regret at the closing of Federal Theater referred to it as a *pioneering* job. .... He wrote-

> Its significance lies in its pointing to the future. The ten thousand anonymous men and women ...who believed in it - their dreams and deeds were not the end. They were the beginning of a people's theater in a country whose greatest plays are still to come.

When I read those words, I took on what I felt was a personal mission promising myself to carry on her pioneering "when I grew up". My urge to become a successful pioneer drove me to devour almost any book on the theater I could find, - its history, the drama, acting, directing, all of it. And I loved reading plays. I found the same pleasure in reading a play that I found in reading a novel. During those two years at City College, I earned $1.50 an hour running the elevator all day on Saturdays in a 38 story office building at 40 Rector Street off Wall Street. With that generous salary, I had enough spending money for lots of 55 cent tickets. The subway was only a nickel then. I became addicted to Broadway. Off-Broadway, of course, had not yet been imagined.

Hallie Flanagan not only turned me on to the living theater; she also turned me on to Gordon Craig, whom she acknowledged as her own inspiration. Gordon Craig was, in a sense, the father of today's modern stage production. The son of the great actress, Ellen Terry, star of the English stage at the turnoff the century, Craig was one of the most important radical reformers in the theater. After reading Flanagan's tribute to Craig, I rushed to the library and devoured Craig's writings. He preached his doctrine of liberating the early twentieth century theater from the deadening restraints of realism and verisimilitude. He demanded a new approach to the art of the theater. He called for a new age in the theater where what we saw on the stage would transcend the merely natural and bring back mystery and mysticism, glamour and poetic exaltation. In his call for reforms, he included all aspects of theater, especially the actor's art and craft, the designer's imagination, the dramatic use of space and of lighting and music. His words were a seductive invitation that converted so many of us who took them to heart. Today's modern theater, in all its aspects, bears witness to the far reaching influence of his passionate preaching.

Recently I came across a citation from Thornton Wilder which is evidence that Gordon Craig's crusade to liberate the theater from the bonds of naturalism must have reached Wilder's ears as it did mine. Here is a comment from a book review, by Jeremy McArthur in the **NYTimes Book Review**, of a recently published **Collected Plays and Writings on Theater** by Thornton Wilder. McArthur wrote, with quotes from Wilder:

The theater's ability to present the universal and eternal made it the greatest of all the arts, but the 19th-century vogue for box sets and realistic props had reduced it to a minor art and an inconsequential diversion. He [Wilder] realized that for theater to regain its old pre-eminence, it would need to abandon naturalism and rediscover the tools of Shakespeare and the Greeks: stage conventions that convey — a marvelous distinction — not verisimilitude but reality. Thus Wilder's lack of scenery and other brazenly theatrical devices are all ways of escaping the literal and picayune, of stretching theater as far as an engaged audience's imagination can take it. The uncanny result is plays that pursue the emotional aims of Chekhov with the adventurous theatricality of Brecht.

The lessons of Flanagan and Craig eventually set me to planning my own grass roots theater company, anti-naturalistic to the core. I knew that, first of all, I needed training, and I went after it.

After two years at City College, with World War II starting up, I took a job as film editor in New York. I worked for a few years on documentary and propaganda films at the Office of War Information in New York and continued to read every play and theater book I could get my hands on. I read all the plays of Shakespeare. I went to almost every opening night on Broadway. A friend taking drama courses at Columbia smuggled me into the lectures of Professor Joseph Wood Krutch, who also served the public as the distinguished theater critic at **The Nation**. We paid $1.10 each to avoid sitting in the very last row of the theater, sending in our combined $2.20 to the box-office on the first Sunday that a new play advertised its opening in the *Times*. How we enjoyed the extravagance! We always went to the opening night; what a thrill as the house lights came down! It still sends shivers down my back and, in these waning years, even tears.

I'm sure my vision of what the theater might be was shaped by the remarkably rich experience of the Broadway theater during and just after the war. In my teaching career, I have never been able to adequately share with my students what it was to have seen and heard the unforgettable and truly great giants of the theater of those days. What comes to mind, as I think back, are Maurice Evans and Mady Christians in splendid Elizabethan costume in the uncut "Hamlet", with a dinner intermission to get us through the almost 5 hour performance. We saw "The Winter's Tale" with Benjamin Iden-Payne directing and acting the role of Autolycus in a production with costumes and sets by Robert Edmond Jones. Unforgettable was Marlon Brando in "Streetcar Named Desire". We were there for the opening night when Katharine Cornell presented the American premiere of the Anouilh "Antigone", and then a few weeks later she did Shaw's Candida", first with Burgess Meredith as Marchbanks, the poet, and then – for a week only – with Marlon Brando in the same role. Ethel Barrymore and her voice resonating with golden tones that still ring in my ears. She spoke the most beautiful and affecting English I've ever heard in all my life. And there were the unforgettable Judith Anderson and Helen Hayes, to name a few more. A most vivid memory of those seasons was the visit to New York during the war by The Old Vic from London, with Lawrence Olivier, Ralph Richardson, and a company of British actors whose theater in London was built not too far from where Shakespeare's Globe Theater had originally stood. The Old Vic sitting in the heart of London wasn't exactly a grass roots theater, but it was certainly a people's theater, a popular theater. It was the Old Vic and the Abbey players that illuminated for me the heights that could be reached by an ensemble performance by a company of actors, playing together season after season.

In 1946, at age twenty-one, I took the historic City of San Francisco trans-continental train from New York to Berkeley, to complete my work for the A.B. degree. At the University of California, Berkeley, I signed on for courses in dramatic literature, Greek and Roman theater, the Elizabethans and Shakespeare, as well as Restoration comedy and modern British and American drama. I plunged into every area of study I could find to broaden my perspective and prepare for my unwavering commitment. I even took a summer course in Speech for the Stage, with visiting Margaret Prendergast McLean, who taught us to drop our local accents, even mine from the Bronx, so we could speak easily, elegantly and naturally, the speech and language of Shakespeare and Oscar Wilde. My friends scorned my new speech, but I persevered. How important that training proved to be in directing my future grass roots company!

I also worked on the college theater productions, hooked by the smell of the hot glue used in the scenery paint we mixed in the shop. I was also hooked by a girl named Suzanna, with her Titian red hair, who painted the sets and eventually married me and joined in the creation of the Company of the Golden Hind, so I didn't need to try it alone.

Henry Schnitzler, who had been director of the *Teater in der Josefstadt* in Vienna before the war, was teaching directing at Berkeley, and his course provided one more step forward in my preparations. Henry, the youngest son of Viennese playwrite Artur Schnitzler, with his rich personal knowledge of pre-Nazi theater in Vienna, taught us the nuts and bolts of directing a play.

After a semester in his class, I decided to apply his teachings to actually staging a play. In a literature course on the eighteenth century we were reading Milton's "Samson Agonistes" – a play in verse not intended to be acted on the stage, but rather to be read as a piece of poetry in dramatic form. I decided to accept what I took as a personal challenge, and put "Samson Agonistes" on the stage. I found a cast among my classmates in the Theater Department, and the lovely Titian-haired Suzanna helped me with the costumes. The setting, after Gordon Craig, consisted of some simple platforms, some black drapes, and a lighting plan based on principles I had picked up from reading Gordon Craig and his Swiss colleague, Adolphe Appia, whom we now know as the father of modern lighting.

The opening music was a taped recording of the cello solo,"Schlomo" by Ernst Bloch played by the cellist Fournier. When we did the three performances in the small 110 seat lecture hall which served as a theater space, it was clear to me that I had found my "bliss" and I determined to follow it wherever it might lead. I knew from that experience that one day I had to have my own theater company; I had no wish to create a showcase nor a training ground for my own talents nor for those of young actors aching for Broadway success. I dreamt of a theater company in the San Francisco Bay Area where I felt sure we were bound to find an audience of students and faculty in its "town and gown" citizenry. I felt sure that a repertory company that would bring classics and modern plays to life would find public support.

By the time I had completed requirements for my Bachelor's degree, I had no doubt that the place to finish my preparations for making the dream come to life was Carnegie Tech in Pittsburgh. The Carnegie Institute of Technology, now called Carnegie-Mellon University, included, along with its first rate School of Engineering, a School of Fine Arts, including painting and sculpture, architecture, music and theater. Historically, Carnegie Tech was the first institution of higher learning to offer university degrees in theater as far back as the 1920's. I applied for admission for their Master of Fine Arts degree. This was 1948. By that time there were a growing number of university theater departments in the United States, but Carnegie Tech enjoyed the reputation as the most important of them all. The theater department, with a teaching staff recruited from professionals experienced in the Broadway theater, gave courses in acting, directing, speech, theater history, costume design and lighting. All of these offerings focused on the graduates' goal of entering the professional theater after training at Tech. Indeed, their success rate for graduates working on Broadway or in Hollywood was the reason for their well earned reputation.

Destiny or Providence was certainly watching over me as I prepared my application to Carnegie Tech. I didn't know that, at the time, they were accepting no more than three candidates per year in the graduate program. Ignorant of the odds, I escaped the reasonable anxiety which I might have suffered waiting for acceptance of my application. One of the faculty members at Berkeley, Marquis deB. Patterson, whose support and encouragement in everything I tried to do was unfailing, was a graduate of Carnegie Tech and his letter of recommendation was pivotal. Before the Fall semester was over, I had a letter confirming my acceptance. Since they accepted new students only once a year in the Fall, I was expected the following September.

By January, 1948, I was finished with all my courses required for the Bachelor's Degree. That gave me time until September to earn some money, see more theater in New York, and ready myself for my mission. During that summer of '48, I was wandering around Times Square one sunny day when I unexpectedly, literally, bumped into Jim Taylor, a classmate from a theater course in Berkeley. Jim had come to New York the year before to make his way on the stage. Delighted as we both were to find each other so accidentally or coincidentally, we brought each other up to date, and Jim told me he had auditioned for the acting program at the Neighborhood Playhouse, the outstanding professional theater school in New York at that time. Sanford Meisner, well known for his important role in creating the famed Broadway Group Theater of the 30's, was teaching the acting course, and Jim had been accepted as a full scholarship student. We had several coffees together with one of "Nathan's Famous" hot dogs at a coffee shop off Times Square.

As we were finishing our lunch Jim asked, "By the way, do you happen to know who Lee Strasberg was?"

"What do you mean was?" I said. "He's still alive I think, not so old. He was one of the principal directors of the Group Theater, along with Stella Adler and your Sandy Meisner. I actually saw some of their plays before they folded. Clifford Odets was their playwright. I saw his "Awake and Sing" with Carnovsky as the old man. "Waiting for Lefty" and "Rocket to the Moon" and .... oh, I forget, ... a few others. I haven't seen his name anywhere for some time.

"If I'm not mistaken," I went on, "it was Strasberg, together with Stella Adler and Meisner, who taught the Group Theater the Stanislavsky approach to acting for which they were well known. Yes, I recall that Stella Adler had spent some time with Stanislavsky, himself, at the Moscow Art Theater. She returned to New York with copious notes of all she had learned, and she shared them with the Group Theater actors when they went off for a summer of working together in the Catskills before stepping out on Broadway. They say that Marlon Brando worked with Stella preparing "Streetcar". What about Strasberg?"

"Well," Jim continued, "he's about to give a course in acting. He's here in New York. He's giving an eight week course for young Broadway actors in the studio space on the top floor of the Theater Guild's Playhouse on 46th Street. The classes will meet once a week for three hours. He's starting next week. Maybe you'd like to come with me?"

"You bet I would." I said. "I've read Clurman's book **The Fervent Years**," all about the Group Theater, their goals and successes, and their disappointments. And how Stella Adler brought them Stanislavsky's words direct from the Master's mouth. I'd love to take a class in acting with Strasberg."

The following week, we met at the Theater Guild Playhouse and I had the thrill of entering through the Stage Door. We climbed the stairs and reached the floor above the stage and auditorium. The studio was a large white room in need of fresh paint. It was at the front of the building with big, bare windows facing 46th street below, too far below to let disturbing street noises reach us. I remember it was a very hot and humid August. There was no air conditioning, and we sat on folding chairs lined up in a few rows facing the bare space where our scenes would be performed. Robert Lewis, who later became an important producer-director on Broadway, was there to collect our fees, paid at the start of every session. I think it was $2.50 per session. None of us had any idea that this was to become the Mecca of the Broadway acting world.

Strasberg sat at a small wooden table in front and to our left. He sat solemnly looking us over. When we all were quiet, he welcomed us briefly and said we'd do scenes from any play of our choice lasting no more than ten or fifteen minutes, and we needed to sign up for the time in advance. After each scene, he said, he would make comments, offer suggestions. But before starting, he wanted to have a few minutes with each one of us to know us better and what work we had done. When it was my turn, I explained that I had just finished my B.A. at Berkeley and was preparing to go to Carnegie Tech in September for a Master's in directing. I said I was sure his class would be invaluable and I was very pleased to join the group.

Strasberg said, "Well, you know these people all have worked on the stage and you haven't had the experience that they bring. I'm wondering if you'll get much out of being here with us. Maybe it's not worth your time?"

I smelled rejection. I answered him, "Mr. Strasberg, I hope you'll let me attend the first session and we'll see. Would you mind? And let me be the judge?"

He smiled faintly at me. I'm sure he knew chutzpah when he saw it. But he was tolerant. He said, "That's O.K. Let's see."

I was not so foolhardy as to sign up to do a scene the very first session.

At the end of that first session, I said to him, "Thank you, Mr. Strasberg. This has been very rewarding for me. I've learned so much from just this first session. I hope you'll let me stay."

He smiled and nodded agreement.

Our classes followed a simple pattern with very little formality. The actors usually volunteered the week before they wanted to go on. We started promptly at 2:00 p.m. and finished by 5:00. One of the actors in each scene announced the play, the scene and the characters, usually no more than two or three. There was never any explanation to orient us. The idea was that when presenting our scene we would, through our performance, convey to the class our intentions, who we were and where we were, and what we were feeling. The key word was "intention". Strasberg always listened with complete attention without interrupting. There was never any applause, of course; we were working, searching, learning, not performing. After each scene he spent thirty to forty minutes in analysis and discussion. First he asked, "Where are you?" and most of us placed the action in general terms, ..."In my mother's house....in the schoolroom.....on a street in Rome". Next he asked "Who are you" with a very probing look so you didn't know if he meant, "Who is this character you're impersonating?" or "Who do you think you are to ask us to pay attention to this scene?" The next question was, "What are you doing here? What's your purpose, your intention?"

Following the responses to these kinds of questions, he began to comment on how well we had created our character, established the reality of the place and credibility in our stated intention. He gave us at least twenty to thirty minutes of his unwavering attention, sometimes restaging the first moments of our scene, to be sure we understood his meaning. His comments were very perceptive and his suggestions helped us make use of our imagination to achieve what we said we were aiming for. He spoke in simple English, no stage jargon, totally sympathetic to our stated intentions, and usually his suggestions were easy to understand and to follow. We valued his comments because we could sense how much he contributed to our acting skills.

I won't try to describe fully the Lee Strasberg teaching process, but there was one comment he made at the first session, which he found reason to repeat on several other occasions, and for me it was a key to his artistic approach which came to be called "method acting". It came after we saw a scene between Stanley and Stella from "Streetcar Named Desire". I recall his comment to the two steamy actors. He said, "You seem to know where you're going with the scene. You're communicating your intentions as the scene starts, but you both seem to be in the grip of your emotions from the very start of the scene. You practically reached your most intense moment at the very beginning of the scene. Where can you go from there? There's no room for you to go anywhere. We get the impression that you're out of control. I mean it's not clear if it's the character that's crossing the line, getting out of control, or the actor. It's as if you're both on the streetcar, and you can't get off."

He then went on to say that creating an authentic emotional state for a scene requires, first of all, a completely credible concentration, so that we believe in the characters' intentions, and in their relationship to each other and in the space in which they breathe. But then we need to sense that the actor is driving the scene and the emotion, and is not being driven by emotions he can't control.

The actors started the scene again, once more "from the top" .This time there was only a suggestion of lust and rage lying dormant in the characters.As the scene went on, these passions erupted as a consequence of the interaction between the characters. For me, and I'm sure for the others in the studio, this lesson proved to be very significant and, indeed, unforgettable.

In the weeks after this session we heard Strasberg repeat, "You're riding the streetcar.You've got to get off it or you'll never get where you want to be at the end of the scene."

During each subsequent class, I sat in utter absorption through the three hours, and resented the fifteen minute break in the middle. We hadn't yet heard about "method acting". Years later, when it became part of the common vocabulary in the American theater, I reminded myself that very often the hysterical high-pitched emotional acting we sometimes see labeled "method acting", is not what I recall of Lee Strasberg's lessons in the studio atop the Theater Guild Playhouse.When I started to direct my own actors, I always recalled those weekly sessions where I learned how to ask the questions about where, and who, and what the actor had in mind, so I could guide them toward being more effective, more truthful.

The summer sessions continued and inevitably the moment came when it was time for my scene. I had the blind and stupid arrogance to prepare the opening monologue delivered by Prometheus in "Prometheus Bound" by

Aeschylus. It was a very hot day and I started perspiring as soon as I took the floor. But that was nothing to what I felt after a few lines. By the time I got to the third line, I knew I was disgracing myself. As if I had soiled my trousers in public! I was so ashamed. I was drenched in sweat. It was what we in the theater call "flop sweat". It's what all actors experience when they know their scene is bad beyond belief. I remember that I thought a hundred times of stopping. I prayed for an earthquake or some other natural disaster to save me from further shame. It was clear to me how bad I was, and that the other actors in the room were embarrassed by my incompetence. I'll never know how I didn't lose my nerve, nor why Strasberg quietly let me finish the fifty or sixty lines. I really wished I were dead.

His first words to me showed respect; he was talking to a serious actor worthy of his serious consideration. He asked me all the questions and guided me toward an understanding of who, where, what I thought about the scene and how to approach achieving what I thought was right. Under his kind and considerate gaze, and engaged by his piercing questions, I realized truly, and profoundly, the value of those questions. I answered as best I could. He encouraged me to speak without reservation, without apology. I spoke as if I were in a confessional. I felt his compassion, his generosity in every word he spoke to me, and I've cherished those words all my life since.

When the session was over, as we got to the street, some of my colleagues in the class expressed sympathy for the raking over they said Strasberg gave me. I tried to tell them how much I learned from his comments and that they were far from a raking over. I learned more that hour than I had learned from any book or acting lesson. I really felt I "got it". I knew what acting was about even if I couldn't do it, couldn't abandon myself to it to the extent I always required later on from the actors I worked with.

Some weeks later, I went on with an actress who had chosen a scene from Tchekov's "Uncle Vanya". We did the scene where Dr. Astrov comes on stage to tell Yelena, the young wife of the old professor, that he loves her. My Dr. Astrov recited words he had composed in advance of what he feared would be an awkward encounter. Strasberg lead me to inhabit the character as I had described him, and to speak from the heart, even if the words came out like an awkward set speech. In fact that's what the scene was really about. The doctor spoke from his heart, but the words he used made him sound like he was reading a too well prepared speech. What a wonderful tension that insight gave the scene.

By the time we got to the sixth week, I had to explain to Strasberg that I regretted terribly that I had to miss the last two sessions and leave for the start of the semester in Pittsburgh. I thanked him for all the insights I had gained, beyond anything I expected. As we shook hands, Lee Strasberg, looked at me and said quite simply, "If you have some questions you'd like to discuss with me about the actor's work, why don't you come up for a coffee at my place before you leave for Carnegie Tech? It won't bother my wife, and it will be pleasant for me as well as you."

I didn't faint. A few days later I saw him at his apartment, in his library. He had the most complete library of books on theater, including plays, history, criticism I had ever seen in one place. I thought to myself he was probably the most erudite person practicing theater in our time.

We talked mostly about acting styles. I can't recall the whole two hours we had together, but I remember discussing with him the performance of Judith Anderson in "Medea" which she had been doing, and comparing it with Marlon Brando in "Streetcar Named Desire". Here were two incomparable examples of the kind of acting we had been reaching for in the class. Actor and actress were each creating an appropriate reality through the medium of these two plays even though they were from two utterly different eras, two different cultures.

What I learned from Strasberg that afternoon was that the reality for the actor lies in the intention which he ascribes to his character. His actor's concentration must be fully focused on that character's intention. Of course, every actor chooses to give to his impersonation of a character an intention that seems to the actor to be true to the circumstances of the play. That's where the word "style" comes in. When we talk about style in acting, we're referring to the actor's body language, the way he walks, the way he talks, his rhythm in movement and speech, the way he relates to the others with whom he interacts, and how he responds to the world in which the play takes place; these are the actor's elements of style. An actor in a Greek tragedy has to find a style which is true to the ancient Greeks, while a driven dock worker in New Orleans, feeling demeaned by his neurotic sister-in-law, has to find a style true to life at the end of the streetcar line.

Style, however, is not a substitute for the truth of intention. That truth comes from the heart. The actor's truth is the intention he identifies in the character; every skillful actor knows that in exposing his character's intention, he's also exposing a part of his own character, his own truth, his own being. (It's hard to put into words, but when you see it on stage, you know it. If you have seen Brando or Judith Anderson, or Vanessa Redgrave or Judy Dench – among others, of course, - you have seen actors in touch with their own truth which is what touches us spectators.)

When I came away from my coffee with Lee Strasburg, I knew I was committed to following his path in conjunction with the direction already pointed out to me by Hallie Flanagan and Gordon Craig. The week after our coffee together I was in Pittsburgh, thrilled to be part of the Carnegie Tech Theater Department.

It was clear to me from the first day at Carnegie Tech that this was a training ground for professionals, run by professionals, where we would learn to become professionals.

The faculty made it clear we were expected to be committed to excellence in all things. We were warned early on that, after finishing our training at Tech, we were going to face an army of competitors as eager and committed as we were to become part of the professional theater. I learned the nuts and bolts of lighting, designing sets and costumes, as well as creating appropriate movements for the actors, and establishing entrances and exits in staging a scene.

The lessons of Flanagan, Craig, and Strasberg I brought with me were tucked away among my books and baggage.

The language of Carnegie Tech included a different kind of vocabulary.

In staging my first production for the directing class, I used everything I had learned before coming to Tech. I chose to do "The Second Shepherds' Play" from the Medieval Wakefield Cycle of plays. My turn came up just before the Christmas break. My school-mates were an attentive and critical audience, a bit surprised, and genuinely moved by the play. These were my peers and their response to the performance was reassuring. Their appreciation was a confirmation that my years of yearning and training were paying off.

Soon after the Christmas break, I accepted a paying job to start up a community theater of young amateurs with little or no training or experience. At the Kaufmann Community Center, a settlement house to serve the inner city, we were a part of their outreach to the community. To my knowledge, and after some research, it appeared to me we were among the first inter-racial community theater groups in the country. This was, after all, 1948-49, years before "affirmative action" and "political correctness" came into common usage. I wanted to give the young actors, black and white, an experience that would liberate them from always confronting the social pressures of their daily life. I chose plays for them unrelated to the racism and poverty and politics of the day. The first play we did was an historic medieval play, "Gammer Gerton's Needle". It's one of the earliest preserved comedies in English, and they did it with such verve it turned out to be a big laugh hit. Next we did a modern comedy about a half dozen young wannabe actors in Greenwich Village who finally make it on Broadway.

I enjoyed working at the Community Center and really needed the salary of several hundred dollars a month. I was ardently planning to join Suzanna in Paris that summer where she planned to be. I had by then decided I wanted her to share in my life and in creating the theater of my dreams.

As it happened, she preceded me to Europe by a few weeks and I had some difficulty in catching up with her. Spurred on by my longings, I booked passage on a student ship, a transport left over from the war, and fitted with cabins to accommodate hordes of students eager to visit Europe on a limited budget. The ship was the "Westerdam" of the Holland America Line. It left from Hoboken and I stood by the railing up on deck to see us slip out of New York Harbor. It was as thrilling as I had imagined it would be. As we were passing the city, a fellow passenger, who seemed a bit older than I, stood by me at the railing and we struck up a casual conversation. "Is this your first trip to Europe?" he asked me.

"Yes, it is," I said.

"Are you a student?" he asked.

"Yes, I am," I replied. "I've just finished my first year of graduate work at Carnegie Tech. I did my Bachelor's Degree at UC Berkeley. And you?"

"I teach in the English Department at Texas A. & M. but I spent the year before last at Berkeley, on my thesis. Were you there that year?"

"Yes, I was, as a matter of fact. That was my last year there." I replied.

"I wonder if you saw what I thought was a very interesting production of Milton's "Samson Agonistes". It was staged by one of the students. You know it's never staged."

I was startled, indeed. "Yes," I said, "I certainly did see that production. In fact I'll confess I'm the one who directed it."

He beamed. "What a coincidence. Let me tell you I liked the production very much. In fact I paid you the very highest compliment. They say imitation is the sincerest form of flattery. Well, I went home to Texas after seeing your production and staged my own production of "Samson Agonistes" at our campus. Isn't it strange that we meet this way? I'm so pleased to be able to congratulate you."

What a way to start my first voyage to Paris, I thought! It raised my expectations for a happy conclusion to my voyage. I wasn't disappointed.

Our courtship, Suzanna's and mine, reads like a script following the formula: boy-meets-girl, boy-loses-girl, and boy gets girl. And it ends happily, like all the scripts do. In Paris I finally tracked down Suzanna and we traveled together the rest of the summer, stopping for a few days at Avignon where we were in time for the now famous Avignon Theater Festival, then in its second season.

From Avignon we went on to sunny Italy, including visits to Rome, Florence, and Fiesole. My proposal of marriage, staged in the afternoon light under the olive trees at Fiesole, was straight from the heart, and she said "Yes." We both agreed on a commitment to creating the grass roots theater which took on more and more reality the more we talked about it.

We returned to Pittsburgh so I could complete my second year there for my Masters Degree. We planned a traditional Jewish wedding in the spring, and then a return to Berkeley to start our work. Fate had it otherwise.

It seems that, during that first winter of 1948 in Pittsburgh, I saw an interesting notice on a bulletin board at Tech with details about what was called the Fulbright Act Scholarship Program for Study Abroad. I sent in an application and didn't give it much thought once it was in the mail. However, soon after we returned to Pittsburgh in September, I was startled to receive a notice that my application for a Fulbright Scholarship had been accepted! I had been granted a stipend to spend a year in France, with courses at the Sorbonne or wherever I wanted. But I had to arrive in Europe in the 1949 calendar year to qualify for the funds. Suzanna agreed we could marry in December and so we did, and returned to Paris without delay.

Is there any better place for a honeymoon than Paris? I doubt it. We spent the year traveling to some of the major cities in Europe, taking in all the theater we could. The Old Vic in London and the Shakespeare Festival in Stratford were high on our list. We also included visits to Vienna, Athens, and Rome.

Paris, for us was a "movable feast" as it had been for Hemingway, and as it had been for so many aspiring artists before and since. We enjoyed the theaters, the museums, and our daily meanderings about the city. But we also enrolled in a class in mime given by Etienne Decroux, who was acclaimed world wide as the supreme master of the art of mime, noted for being the teacher of Jean-Louis Barrault and Marcel Marçeau among others.

We heard that the aging Olga Preobajenska, one of the original five prima ballerina's of the Tzar's Ballet Russe, had retired to Paris and was giving classes in classical ballet in a studio in the Salle Wagram on the Avenue de Clichy. Suzanna, who had been taking modern dance classes in San Francisco while a student at UC Berkeley, made a point of taking classes with Mme. Preobajenska for several months before our travels interfered. As the proud husband of the "American" (as Madame called Suzanna) I was able to watch the classes, always with pleasure. The classes with Decroux and Preobajenska added some extra insight to our understanding of movement on the stage.

However, there's no question in my mind that the most meaningful contribution to our preparations for our new theater came from a regional theater company called *La Comédie de St. Etienne*, based in the city of St. Etienne, serving the entire Southeast of France. Its full name, translated into English, was the National Theater Center for the Southeast.

At the end of the war the French Department of Culture under the direction of André Malraux decided to decentralize the French theater which, until then, had hardly existed outside Paris. Malraux wanted to do for France, I learned, what Hallie Flanagan had done for America. I don't know if he was even aware of her work. But his project was almost a mirror image of hers, but with its inimitable French flair.

La Comédie was one of four regional companies set up in the four main regions of the country. St. Etienne was the Pittsburgh of France and was the logical center for its region. The company's home was at the National School of Mines in the heart of the city. It was given space to set up a rehearsal stage, workrooms for building sets, sewing costumes, and pursuing all the different activities necessary to a regional theater. The company of fourteen or sixteen actors and some technical staff prepared each production in St. Etienne and then performed in the surrounding cities and towns, doing mostly one-night stands in movie houses, town halls, school auditoriums and the like. The space they were given at the School of Mines made it possible not only to work on the production and rehearse, but also to take their meals all together as a family. In effect the work space itself contributed much to creating the ensemble acting that the director, Jean Dasté, was after.

My friend, Paul Arnold, in Paris, who published a monthly French theater magazine, had assured me that the most interesting theater work in France at that moment was taking place in St. Etienne. Paul insisted that I must plan to spend some time with Dasté and he gave me a letter of introduction. When I explained to Dasté that we were about to launch a regional theater in San Francisco, he invited us to follow whatever activities they were engaged in, as we wished; to come and go wherever our fancy lead us.

His mostly young actors came from Paris, agreeing to spend a whole year in the industrial heartland performing a repertoire of six productions, from Molière to LaBiche and the modern playwright Anouilh. One of his actors,

René LaForgue, was also a composer and arranged music for the stage. He acted, composed, and served as the music director for the company. He insisted that every one in the company sing the music he arranged for the production, and we were so taken by his use of music to enhance the action that we followed his example when we went into production in California. Suzanna and I recalled later on how we laughed to hear René shout at the actors,

"Louder, louder! I can't hear you. Don't tell me you have no voice for singing. God gave you a voice for singing. That's how he made us all. So sing. Sing. Sing!"

Each production of theirs played its first two or three performances in St. Etienne, followed by a tour of the surrounding Southeast towns which contributed tax revenue to support the company. We were invited to join them on tour for a week or ten days during our visit. For the tour we all traveled in two buses, adapted to carry, along with the company members, the costumes in huge wicker trunks. The sets and lighting were designed to be portable and to be easily folded and carried in the space in the rear of both buses. We took notice that whether they were rehearsing at their home at the School of Mines or on the road, we all ate lunch and dinner together, as a family. And everyone, including Suzanna and me, had an extra mid-day hour for a siesta or a walk or a quiet time, as we wished. Music rehearsals usually took place after the siesta.

On the road, once the company arrived at their destination, we all worked to assemble the set, hang the lights, iron the costumes and organize the dressing and make-up rooms. The day was quite full, since the buses usually started up in St. Etienne precisely at 8:00 a.m. and the driving could last anywhere from an hour and a half to almost three hours. The return to St. Etienne every evening after the performance found everyone asleep, curled up as best they could in the buses.

Living and traveling with the company was wonderfully inspiring and energizing for Suzanna and me. As our visit continued in the heart of the *Comédie de St. Etienne*, our theater company-to-be began to reveal itself to us. I decided I wanted to create a regional theater company that would be for the San Francisco Bay Area what *La Comédie de St. Etienne* was for the southeast of France.

Arriving in Berkeley in the Fall of 1950 after our Fulbright year in Europe, we had no money, not even a job between us, but we had our dream. To keep a roof over our heads, we took odd jobs for the mornings so we could spend the rest of the day and evening on our theater project. My first job was as a delivery man for a bakery bringing bread, rolls and baked goods to the fraternities and sororities around the campus. I started work at 5:00 a.m. and was free by 10:00 . Suzanna got a job at a print shop where the printer, an elegant Englishman, hired her part-time to keep books, deliver print jobs, and be a general shop assistant while he played cricket with the local cricket club in Golden Gate Park. He was charmed by her, and who wasn't?

After some months, I started to work for better pay as a conductor on the interurban train, the F train, between Berkeley and San Francisco, crossing the bay on the Bay Bridge. A few months later I started teaching sub-Freshman

English at U.C. with my first class at 8:00 a.m., but I kept the conductor's job for a while because we needed the money. Fortunately, I had a schedule that started on the train at 5:45 a.m. and, after two round trips, my schedule was over and I could leave the train on the edge of campus at 7:45 a.m. This was just in time for me to put my train conductor's cap and change-carrier into my briefcase, and walk up on campus to my first class at 8:00 a.m. Often I would collect fares from riders coming from San Francisco who were also students in my 8:00 o'clock. We always laughed together when they saw me put my gear into my briefcase and put on my professorial face.

Suzanna and I talked about our theater company every waking moment. I was busy reading plays and searching in my imagination for an entry into that wonderland of theater I had dreamed about. We were looking for "a local habitation and a name." to quote the Bard.

One day, I woke up and said to Suzanna, "Did you know that when Sir Francis Drake sailed from England to San Francisco Bay in his ship, The Golden Hind, he had a half dozen actors with him and they performed plays to keep his officers in good spirits?"

"You don't say," said Suzanna, rather quizically. "Are you making that up?"

"Certainly not. It's all true. I read about it yesterday in a book on Drake's voyage here. I think we should make a spiritual connection here on San Francisco Bay with Drake's company of actors and call ourselves The Company of the Golden Hind. Let's say we are the natural heirs of those actors who sailed with Drake and his officers."

"Yes, I like it," Suzanna said with conviction. "The Company of the Golden Hind" . That's a name that suits our intentions, our decision to put down our roots."

II - GRASS ROOTS SPROUTING

The grass roots Company of the Golden Hind actually sprouted in the unlikely corner of an asphalt covered parking lot in Berkeley, California. Soon after our return from France, Suzanna and I had rented a small two bedroom cottage on Channing Way, five minutes from Sather Gate, the main entrance to the campus. The cottage dated back to the beginning of the century. Since it included the original indoor bathroom, we guessed it was built around World War I. It was located at the rear of a parking lot adjoining a small one story, newly built brick building housing two dental offices. Our cottage sat up against a six foot wall covered with climbing nasturtium and wild blackberries which Suzanna brought to our table.

The two bedrooms were small, but we had a fair sized living room and a large farmhouse kitchen with an old wood-and-coal burning stove that had been fitted with gas burners. Although the oven also continued to work, we were told, on wood or coal as well as gas, we never tested it. In the wooden shed attached to the side of our house sat an ancient hot water heater, dating back to the same year the bathroom was installed. Made of decorative

cast iron, it sprang to life when you struck an old fashioned kitchen match to light the coil of gas jets just inside
the round iron door. We quickly learned to swing open
the small iron door to the heater with a sharp jerk of the
tiny handle. We lived with the daily fear it would blow
up unexpectedly, so we were very judicious in turning on
the gas heater for hot water, saving it for bathing, morning shaving, and doing the dishes. However, we began
to feel more and more fortunate about our find as we
began putting our theater project together, using the kitchen
table for costume construction and props. The parking lot,
always empty on evenings and week-ends, served us splen-
didly for space where we could build our sets without
interruption.

Our strategic plan to bring the Company of the Golden
Hind to life faced three major challenges. First, we needed
to be clear about our identity as The Company of the
Golden Hind, and about our mission. Then, there were the
nuts and bolts of organizing the logistics of production.
Last, we faced the challenge of choosing a play and mount-
ing it on stage.

Rehearsals couldn't begin until I found a place to rehearse as well as a theater or performance space. Almost
simultaneously, we faced the challenges of designing the
sets, costumes and props, placing ads in the local papers,
printing programs and posters for the shop windows
around Sather Gate at U.C. and creating a production budget including rental charges for rehearsal and performance
space. Finally, we were face-to-face with the need to find
the money to pay for it all.

Our mission was clear to us. Wherever we went, we talked up our goal of establishing a truly grass roots regional theater which would be a worthy descendant of that troupe of actors Sir Francis Drake brought with him on his flagship, the Golden Hind, when it first sailed into San Francisco Bay. We tried to describe our lofty mission as modestly as we could, though it was clear to everyone we talked to that it was an impossible dream. We gave little importance to the fact that in 1951 there were only three other small resident companies in the Bay Area, and we would be the fourth. We spoke with conviction of the dormant theater audience we would soon arouse by our productions. We saw the Company of the Golden Hind, in good time, becoming a professional, paid, Equity company.

I even had the chutzpah in my conversations with almost everyone to whom we talked to say that we were inspired by Molière. In seventeenth century France, Molière left Paris with his mistress and a small traveling company *Le Théâtre Illustre, (The Illustrious Theater).* The company grew to become one of the great theatrical institutions of Europe, and has continued to perform without interruption (except for war), even until today, as the National Theater of France. It's called *La Comédie Française.* More stable than any of the governments of France, it has survived the French revolution, is still self-governing, and has continued to flourish through the five republics and First and Second Empires which replaced the monarchy of Molière's day. It is certainly the oldest continuously running theater in the world, and, I, immodestly, suggested to the Bay Area public that we were seeking to establish for the San Francisco Bay, a theater with *La Comédie Française* as our model.

I repeated over and over again to company members as we recruited them through the years, as well as to the press and public, one basic premise: our San Francisco theater was not to serve as a stepping stone or a preparation before hitting the "big time" on Broadway. I had no idea how long it would be before we could put the company on a professional paying basis, but from the start we were committed to the long term. We were looking forward to staging plays from the entire repertoire, reaching back to the Greeks and proceeding through the Elizabethan drama into the twentieth century, including plays drawn from every country and culture. Most important was our commitment to the anti-naturalistic theater concepts received directly from our mentors, the British Gordon Craig and our American Thornton Wilder. (We learned very soon that Wilder had graduated from our own Berkeley High; in fact, in later years I actually met his sister, Isabel, on one of her visits to old friends from her days at Berkeley High.)

Suzanna and I agreed on one important and overriding principle to guide us in our choice of repertoire. We were in total agreement that our plays had to celebrate the human condition. Celebrate is the operative word. The play did not have to come to a happy ending. We insisted, however, that each production, whether comic or tragic, must be one in which the human spirit achieves affirmation, exaltation, or even redemption before the final curtain. We also included in our mission the exhortation of Gertrude Stein who said, "It is the function of the artist to be exciting."

To this statement of our artistic mission I added, "... and to be illuminating and entertaining as well." When it came to the creative process of staging a production that illuminated and entertained, the words of Oscar Wilde flashed before our eyes: "In matters of importance, style not sincerity is the thing."

This is not to say that sincerity, in the sense of being true to the character, is not important. Rather, we started by first creating the reality of each character. Then, with Wilde looking over our shoulder, we searched for those elements of style that would positively enhance and project with meaning what we understood to be the playwright's intentions.

As we proceeded in rehearsal, we found our way to creating what we called our "dramatic metaphor". The dramatic metaphor, which grew out of our interpretation of the play, could be called the central controlling idea of the production. It determined for us what the style should be for uniting all production elements: staging, acting, setting, costumes, even lighting and make-up. From our very first season, The Company of the Golden Hind became known for the creative imagination evident in the various styles with which we mounted our productions. Chapter Four will detail how we came to this concept of a dramatic metaphor and what were some of the most successful metaphors which we employed during our ten years of production.

Before we could begin to live up to what we professed as our mission, we had some heavy lifting to do, including what I referred to above as the nuts and bolts of production.

Looking for a stage and a rehearsal space, I heard that Berkeley High had a pleasant little 640 seat theater which might suit our performances. The city allowed rental of the theater to non-profit groups for performances or meetings, and I found to my delight, that we could rent the theater for $150 per night, reduced to $100 on the nights of tech and dress rehearsals.

In 1950 the City of Berkeley made it abundantly clear what a warm-hearted community it was. No one asked me for a deposit check when I signed the contract with the high school administration, reserving two weekends, Friday and Saturday evenings, plus two dress rehearsals previous to the first performance. I was told my check for a deposit was required no later than two weeks before the performances, and the balance due was payable after each weekend set of performances. Here was an unexpected blessing since we didn't have enough in our personal bank account to pay even the deposit at the signing. Suzanna thought I was deranged to sign, knowing we didn't have a dime. She was so upset, she wouldn't even hear my rationale and my illusions (some might say delusions), about our anticipated success. I was so self- assured in fact, I would have signed my life away. I was dead certain that our ticket sales would positively keep us from going to jail, or whatever they did to people who signed contracts without means.

As you'll see, the Gods were with us. How lucky we were to be in benevolent Berkeley.

It so happened that the high school also let community groups have a class room free of charge on weekday evenings from 7:00 p.m. to 10:00 p.m. for meetings or, as in our case, for rehearsals. I learned that we were the only group which met to rehearse a play. Indeed, at the time, we were the only theater group in Berkeley except for the Theater Department at the University of California. To make use of the classroom assigned to us, we had to stack all the chairs at the back of the room to have space for staging, and this continued until we got through our first season and half of our second. It was tedious but we did it with a light heart.

Once rehearsal and performance spaces were settled, I strolled down to the offices of **The Berkeley Gazette**, the only paper in town. There I met the charming lady who wrote the entertainment as well as the obituary columns. Entertainment included concerts, films, as well as flea markets, and any other activities in Berkeley that might conceivably amuse or entertain. She was warmly enthusiastic about our starting up a theater company in town. She had had some experience on the stage of her community theater in Sacramento where she grew up, and asked if she could audition for our first production.

With all my heart I promised her she could. She generously printed the announcement of our auditions in the daily **Gazette**, rather closer to the Entertainment columns than the Obituaries. Evidently she thought twice about restarting her acting career because she never showed up at our auditions.

The first production of The Company of the Golden Hind was Shakespeare's "Comedy of Errors". The auditions drew a fair number of actors. Some were friends from undergraduate days, some were students currently enrolled in the theater department, and some were members of the community, working at a variety of jobs: a nurse, a teacher, an insurance agent, a social service worker, a student preparing for his Master's Degree. Almost half had had some acting training or experience. Some had experience acting occasionally with the several community theater groups scattered through towns and cities around San Francisco Bay. Some were would-be actors, friends of friends who had spoken about this new group with the odd, if catchy name, The Company of the Golden Hind. After two days of auditions, I felt I had enough candidates with varying degrees of training and experience to put together a good workable cast. In the principal roles were people from my student days at the UC Theater Department, including one of my best friends whom I knew to be a fine actor,: George Angelo Marchi. It was George who had played the role of Samson Agonistes in that production which attracted the notice of the teacher from Texas mentioned in Chapter One.

The choice of our very first play was certain to be seen as prophetic by us and by the public. It fulfilled our promise to include at least one Shakespearean play in each season. It also suggested the kind of production you could expect to see each time you came to our theater, since even for the first production, we had a dramatic metaphor in mind, and a very distinctive style.

We chose "The Comedy of Errors," a play about identical twins, separated at birth, who find themselves mistaken for each other, while each is unaware that his twin is alive and well and in the same town at the same time. Suzanna agreed with my choice.

My research, prior to making the selection, persuaded me that "Comedy of Errors" was one of Shakespeare's earliest comedies, and historical records indicated it maintained its popularity over time. I took it to be an auspicious choice as a starter for our new company. Furthermore, the production called for a boisterous youthfulness and vigor that seemed to me a welcome challenge for our young company. As we planned it, it would not require expensive costumes nor an elaborate set. I wanted to see the production as an almost improvised comedy performed by a group of circus clowns, with a lot of raucous, boisterous bluster. Suzanna and I decided to create a whole cast of clown-characters, each with its own clown identity. By using stylized clown make-up, we could paint the identical clown face on each set of twins to make the mistaken identity more credible. Suzanna dreamt up a set of circus costumes that had a touch of the Elizabethan era. To further underline the identity of the twins, one from Syracuse and the other from Ephesus, her costumes all followed a color scheme that allowed her to dress one set of characters, all from Syracuse, in alternating green and golden yellow stripes and decorations, while the other set of characters, all from Ephesus, was dressed in mirror images of the same costumes but with red alternating with the golden yellow. It gave the whole stage picture a cheerful look and visual energy that pulled actors and audience together into a truly magical clown-world.

To place the characters in an environment where their shenanigans would be credible and suited to their style, we created a set which, with a bare minimum of décor, suggested the interior of a circus tent, with two sets of platforms, and two sets of banners exploiting the green and gold, or red and gold color identifications. To summarize, the "Comedy of Errors" was staged as if it were a kind of circus clown act.

We took six weeks to rehearse the play, meeting three times a week for five weeks and then every night of the week starting the Monday before our Friday opening. No one was on salary but each actor accepted his role with a completely professional commitment as if they were under contract, and all rehearsals started on time.

At our very first reading, I pronounced the company's "house rules". I made it clear from the start that we were not a cooperative. There was only one director, self-appointed: me. Our company designer was Suzanna and we worked as well as lived together. She designed the set, costumes and make up, and we did the lighting together. We were not open to working by committee and we were not looking for suggestions, however well meaning, from company members.

Criticism by one member of another member was not acceptable, and actors had no voice in the execution of the costumes, just as crew members were encouraged to voice judgments about the actors only if it were to heap praise!

Taking our cue from the *Comédie de St. Etienne,* I persuaded Donald Aird, director of the Berkeley Chamber Singers, to come to a rehearsal and consider teaching our reluctant actors to sing á la St. Etienne's René LaForgue. Happily, Donald was enchanted when he saw a working rehearsal, even before he saw costumes and makeup. He agreed to teach the cast to sing in four part harmony, and I scheduled music rehearsals obligatory for everybody, including me and Suzanna. He was relentless, and achieved wonders with actors with no previous musical experience. I inserted into the production old English roundelays, drinking songs and glees. Even the actors were astonished at how well they did, once they learned the music. In most of the productions which followed, they sang without grumbling, simply for the joy of singing.

Vocal training was not the only training the actors were treated to. St. Etienne had made its mark on me, and I was faithful to it. We arranged for the actors to have some modern dance training to enhance their movement on stage. The modern dance group in San Francisco led by Welland Lathrop and Anna Halpern had a teaching program, and we arranged for Welland to give our actors a weekly class for which we paid the fees. In addition I began most rehearsals with a half hour class in speech for the stage, profiting from my classes with Margaret McLean at U.C. We also worked on the technique for phrasing the Shakespearean language so that a modern audience could understand it, but without sacrificing its poetic richness. When it came to directing the actors in their roles, I called on my experience with Lee Strasberg in those very rewarding sessions in the studio atop the Theater Guild Playhouse.

The Company of the Golden Hind was not a theater conservatory, a school for training would-be actors. Season after season, however, we saw a steady growth in our actors' skills and in our production polish. The same actors who began in "The Comedy of Errors" were ready, after four or five seasons, to accept the challenges of "King Lear" and T.S. Eliot's "Murder in the Cathedral". Critics and the audience responded with generous acknowledgement.

Suzanna's costumes were a real triumph, both for their imaginative concept and the Herculean labors they demanded from her and her devoted sewing team. We did not ever again try to repeat the arduous process Suzanna followed in making the costumes for this first production. She insisted on having the color scheme under control just as we had planned; so to satisfy her artistic demands, as well as our pressing financial limitations, we bought, as I remember, 600 yards of unbleached muslin,--- yes, 600 yards --- at Sears Roebuck, with a newly opened Sears account. We were able to buy aniline dyes from a chemist in San Francisco and then, at home in our little cottage, she mixed her own dyes, boiled the water on our old stove and cooked (should I say dyed !), those 600 yards so that she had fabric of her chosen colors to make the costumes. It was certainly an unforeseen blessing to find a number of women who came to the auditions and said they would love to sew the costumes even if there was no role for them on stage. We had a team of four or five costumers. One of them, a professional designer of women's wear, was enthralled by Suzanna's sketches, and had the expertise to know just how to do the very important cutting, creating her own patterns.

About three weeks before our opening, set for Friday, October 13, 1951, - how could I forget? ,- Suzanna's mother (and therefore my mother-in-law), Helen Hoisington Hart, with a will of steel and a heart of gold, came up from her quiet and elegant home in Long Beach, California, to help sew the costumes and keep our spirits up. Luckily we had the second bedroom which she accepted with good grace. She even cooked for us, she, who had had a live-in cook all her married life.

A few days after her arrival, she asked me how I was getting along with the money to pay for everything. I admitted that I had opened charge accounts everywhere, not only at Sears Roebuck, but also with the hardware store and lumber yard in Berkeley down by the bay. I suppose my earnestness, or my youthful zest accounted for my being accepted as credit worthy. In fact, by then I was teaching as a low level instructor at U.C. and Suzanna held on to her morning job at the print shop for the first two seasons, so we had some kind of steady income.

Helen cleared her throat, as if to say something important. "You know, Rachmael, Harry [her deceased husband] left me with some good oil stocks, and I just got another small dividend I wasn't expecting this month. I could let you have, say, three hundred dollars; wouldn't that help? And then you could put your entire mind into getting this show together, and Suzie and I will see that the costumes are ready. Brownie, who's building your sets certainly seems to have a good head on his shoulders, so we know he'll be ready. You can pay me back when you get on your feet after the show goes on. I just know it'll be a great success."

I didn't hesitate a minute to accept her generosity.

The fact is Helen was a widow in her late sixties when she chose to come up from southern California to help us get our first production together. She had moved from her home in Wichita, Kansas, to Long Beach, California, with her younger sister Peg a few years before we started up. A devoted Presbyterian, she was much involved in the activities of her church in Long Beach, but she found the lure of our theater irresistible.

"Why would I want to live an uneventful life of boredom in my fancy house in Long Beach, in front of the television set, with my woolen throw over my shoulders when I could be part of this exciting life in Berkeley, staying up all night sewing, with you kids?" I heard her say to one of our sewing women one evening as they sweated over the hems for one of Suzanna's more voluminous costume skirts.

The company members knew that Suzanna grew up in Kansas, so they assumed she was a farmer's daughter. They also conjectured that her mother must have been a farmer's wife. But they were puzzled by Helen's grand manner once she arrived. Nevertheless, one of the actors got her to talk about her growing up in Kansas, and her annual visits to New York . These were a special gift from her parents when, as a young woman, she was studying voice and took inspiration from the concerts and the opera season. We were thrilled to hear her stories about those seasons in New York. We were hypnotized when she told us about the night she was in the audience at the Metropolitan Opera when Caruso collapsed on the stage. I called her Helen, Suzanna called her "Mother", but the actors called her "Maw" with a chortle as if she really were a farmer's wife. After the Caruso story, Russ, one of our actors, said

"Gee, we can't call you 'Maw' after your living it up in New York that way."

But Helen said, "No, go on with 'Maw'. After all I am from Kansas, and I love the sound of it with your phony mid-western twang." And we all laughed.

She became the company's den mother and was always ready with a cup of coffee, or a cheerful encouraging word for anyone who looked to her to be in need of one. She never stinted in sending out an actor, cash in hand, for a few dozen hamburgers and cokes to nurture us through a too long rehearsal. Her sometime bossy manner would occasionally clash with my own. We both knew I was the director. But that didn't stop her, and I was polite enough to hear her out with some considered comment or suggestion on the staging, or a lighting effect I was working on. But I didn't appreciate any help, at least not in those early days. I eventually formed a stock reply to her unwelcome assist and we developed a kind of good natured vaudeville routine.

I would say, "Helen, I don't agree with all that. I've got my own idea how I want to do this. Really! Why do you have to sound off like some old battle axe every once in a while?"

Her reply was always, "Rachmael, I know it's none of my business. But you know I'm just too old to change." And we'd both burst out laughing. Helen was a benevolent presence in the Company of the Golden Hind, and even if she couldn't really cook, she was the truly nurturing presence we needed and counted on.

Ready or not, "The Comedy of Errors" was finally about to be performed in front of a live audience. Suzanna had studied graphic design, among other things, and she did wonders in laying out my texts for our advertising, posters and programs. Everyone in the company accepted some responsibility for distributing our publicity to shop windows, friends, PTA meetings, all over town. Our opening night arrived, Friday the 13th of October, 1951. I did not feel we were tempting Fate by accepting that date. In any case, we had no choice since the high school theater teacher always had priority for any dates she wanted the theater for the school play. So when I went to book the theater in the Fall, October 13th was the offer, and October 13th is what I took. Of course with my indomitable optimism I knew it would be a lucky day for us and I was right.

I'll never forget that opening night, even after the dozens and dozens that followed. We had worked through our technical and dress rehearsals the evenings before, with my usual shouting and occasional rages when things did not go smoothly. It was a fair dress rehearsal, with lots of minor snafus. But theater tradition always reminds us that a disappointing dress rehearsal means a glorious opening night performance.

It was 7:00 o'clock on opening night, and Helen and I were alone on the stage with the curtain up, the doors still closed. The actors were working on the stylized clown makeup Suzanna had sketched out for each of them. I wanted no curtain so that the entire theater space was shared by actors and audience, with no barrier between them. Helen had on an old blue apron tied around her waist to protect her clothes as she helped the actors prepare for "lights up" at 8: 30 p.m. Looped around her neck was a tape measure and in her hand a needle and thread so she could make a few adjustments to fitting a costume or two. We both turned to look out at the 640 expectant empty seats in the orchestra and small balcony. We looked into each other's eyes as if we were fellow conspirators, but there was love between us, too. Then we hugged each other. I think that was the first time, in fact the only time, Helen and I hugged each other that I can remember. I said to her, "Well, Helen, we made it." She stepped back to look at me, squarely and seriously. No smile for the moment.

"Yes, Rachmael, you made it. Yes, you did it." And then she smiled, waved her hand in the air and went back stage to fuss over the actors.

I think every theater person knows the shiver that actors and directors feel at that "magic time" on the stage, facing the empty theater on opening night. It's a moment when we are touched by the Gods. I can feel that shiver down my spine even now, recalling that moment.

That night I felt we were a winning team and I needed to give the company some words of acknowledgement of our success as a team. I called everyone together to a corner back stage and gave them a brief pep talk. I told them about how much we had achieved, how much the audience anticipated, and how joyful and promising the evening was going to be for us all. I ended with a rousing , "So go out there and give 'em Hell!"

With an open stage, I had chosen to have Suzanna, an accomplished recorder-flute player, sit on the stage in her "Comedy" costume, feet dangling over the side, while she played music of Shakespeare's period as the public came in to their seats. At 8:30, I stepped out onto the stage. Taking my cue from the customary practice of Jean Dasté at *La Comédie de St. Etienne*, I spoke for just a few minutes as host, welcomed the public to the opening night performance of our new company, and then left the stage to the actors. The Duke of Ephesus made his entrance with the rest of the cast following him, all of them dressed in those 600 yards of hand dyed fabric Suzanna had created with her crew. The audience was stunned to see such a richly costumed cast in a struggling local company's first production. They listened well, they applauded energetically at the end, and we were on our way.

The choice of "The Comedy of Errors" proved to be a good choice to introduce us to the town-and-gown public we expected. Someone from the UC English faculty saw our first performance and, in time for the second weekend, sent out a mimeographed memo (that was some time before Zerox) to inform the faculty that a new theater company of young actors was performing "The Comedy of Errors" in an unusual and "some would say controversial" style. The production might not please everybody, it went on, but it was said to be lively and imaginative. On the other hand, the Theater Department ignored the production, even though more than half of us were former students of the department. From the first, some of the faculty members of the Theater Department were hostile to our goals and our productions for reasons not immediately apparent. It was suggested to me that I had not consulted nor asked for advice and counsel from the chairman nor any other faculty member, and they took that to be a sign of vaunting arrogance. Essentially, we were told, the head of the department thought the stylization, as he heard about it, was "excessive" (his word). I was too excited by our efforts to give it a second thought.

I learned a lot about Shakespeare and his genius from this first staging of one of his plays. I had read and studied them all as a student, and thought I had a good understanding of them. But not until I actually came to prepare a production and bring it to life on the stage did I reach a deeper understanding of what his work was all about. To stage the play, I had to determine on a relevant interpretation. As I began, I had a hunch there was what some call a "sub-text", some meaning, some intention on the part of the playwright, that was the engine that propelled the action and lead to the reconciliation of the twins, to their waking up to each other, - and that I was missing it.

I had to decide what I thought was the "dramatic action", and then express that by means of an appropriate "dramatic metaphor". After much thought and immersion in the text, I had an intuition that struck me. There was a mystery about the play's enduring vitality through the centuries. It wasn't until the evening before our first reading of the play with the cast that my intuition spoke up and Shakespeare's genius that underlies the hilarious fun in "The Comedy of Errors" woke me up in rather a curious way.

Reading through the play a number of times before starting rehearsals, to get it under my skin, as it were, I thought to examine its origin in the Roman comedy by Plautus on which it is acknowledged to be based. Plautus called his play "The Twin Menaechmi". I saw that Shakespeare's characters have comic dimensions and intriguing speeches which go beyond Plautus. Shakespeare gives us not one set of twins, but two sets of twins, separated at birth, who, at the same time find themselves, and the long lost parents of one set, by good or ill fortune, in the city of Ephesus. The comedy shows them completely unaware of each other's existence, with each of them taken by mistake for his twin brother. What makes for the comic in the play is the fact that neither one has any idea of the source of the confusion. Mistaken identity is a common theme in the dramatic action of innumerable comedies throughout history, so at first I thought nothing of it. After a few readings, however, I was struck by the fact that the Roman play by Plautus takes place in the city of Epidamnus, while Shakespeare places his action in Ephesus. I remember wondering aloud about this to Suzanna and her mother.

We were at dinner one evening, and I remarked that , "To me the dramatic action of "Comedy of Errors" is the transformation experienced by each of the main characters, each of the twins. They start out in a state of being ignorant of each other's existence. By a series of "errors", each of them finally discovers that he is not alone in the world. They each discover each other and each one comes to know and welcome the truth that in this world he has a brother." I said.

Helen spoke up, "It sounds serious, almost too serious for a comedy."

"What do you make of that, Suzanna?" I asked.

"Well," she said, "is that the way the play reads, or are you making it up to suit your precious preconceptions?"

"Nonsense," I snorted, "preconceptions, huh! It's all in the text. And it's almost all from Plautus; but Shakespeare's genius adds more interesting characters and hilarious lines. One thing I don't understand is why Shakespeare moved the action from Plautus's Epidamnus to the city of Ephesus. What in the world is there about Ephesus that could have intrigued him?"

With that, Helen, who, incidentally, was a much beloved Sunday School teacher at her Presbyterian church in Wichita, spoke up. "Rachmael, you've never heard of Ephesus?" she asked.

I thought a moment, "You mean the Ephesus of St. Paul and his Letter to the Ephesians?"

"Yes, I do.' she replied. "I mean that exactly. Those are among his most important teachings. What have they to do with Shakespeare's comedy?"

I said, "I don't know St. Paul as you do. What do you think?"

"I guess we'll have to have a look at what St. Paul has to say," she said. And we did. As usual, Helen had her bible with her and showed me the Letter to the Ephesians in the New Testament. I looked up Ephesus in the Biblical Encyclopedia, and what a revelation I found. It was from Ephesus that Paul preached the good news that Jesus came to teach the whole world that all men are brothers. Until then, Christianity was entirely a Jewish sect, its doctrines not addressed to the Gentiles. The Letter to the Ephesians announces that the good news of the coming of the Christ is to be shared with the Gentiles as well. In just so many words, Paul preaches a new brotherhood of man. In this new age, all men are now brothers, if only they will open their eyes and hearts to recognize this eternal truth.

Precisely that is the underlying meaning and Shakespeare's intention in "The Comedy of Errors". Comparing the text of "Comedy of Errors" with the language in Paul's Letter to the Ephesians, I found a striking amount of similarities as well as speeches in which Shakespeare paraphrases the very words of St. Paul.

The last lines of the play sum it up perfectly for St. Paul, I thought. The twins finally wake up; they see the light. As they go out to celebrate their happy reunion at dinner, each insists with courtesy, that the other go first, until one, paraphrasing St. Paul, says to his brother,

"We came into the world as brother and brother.

Let us now go hand in hand, not one before the other."

III - A Local Habitation

With the opening of "The Comedy of Errors," I was obliged and eager to wake from my dream-state and take responsibility for making it come true. It was a joyful awakening. Every morning, seven days a week I would bound out of bed eager to resolve whatever issues were lying in wait for me. There was no one to turn to. No one to ask for advice and counsel, no one to whom I could delegate any of the day's challenges. I realized very quickly, surely out of necessity, that the best course was to welcome each daily crisis, and to expect a successful resolution. The overriding objective was to bring our plays to life, so that our audience would appreciate our productions, understand our intentions, and agree to enter into a state of mind described by the nineteenth century critic, Coleridge as "the willing suspension of disbelief". For me that meant my directing, would be intent on teaching the actors to create their characters, and through their performance articulate the meaning of the play, its interpretation. With Lee Strasberg's wise words ringing in my ears, I focused on the word **intention;** - specifically, the intention of the playwright and the intention motivating each character. The design for the stage set had to be laid out so that the floor plan would be functional, it would facilitate the staging, the acting out of the events occurring in the play. I reminded the whole company that Shakespeare in his own time enjoyed an immense success though he had nothing like the stage, stage machinery, lights, and costumes that we have today. He called upon the imagination of the actors, and of the audience to join in a collaboration in bringing his plays to life, and so would we.

A really vexing problem in carrying out this process was that, in rehearsing in a school classroom, we were always on the classroom floor using the placement of folding chairs to suggest space demarcations and set pieces for standing, sitting, and moving around. All the actors had to work with were the sketches of the set designer, and they did their best to follow the movements I blocked out for them. They had to use their actor's imagination to see the walls, the entrances onto the stage, the steps, the levels, the thrones, the parapets, the furnishings. Only when we took to the stage and had the set pieces of our decor in place, would they be able to work with the real three dimensional setting. With only three stage rehearsals before opening night, we had to cope with one of the most demanding challenges imaginable to get on with the show. I'm happy and proud to report that everyone just accepted our conditions like veterans, eager and ready to move from the classroom floor to the stage.

Costumes were less of a problem since we could make do and rehearse with costume pieces as they were readied;

and long before dress rehearsals we could help them get used to unfamiliar clothing and accessories. With pieces of unbleached muslin Suzanna would fashion a rehearsal train or fake some dragging Medieval sleeves and pin them onto the actor's every day rehearsal clothing, and the plan worked out well.

The lighting was planned in advance, and the lights, never in great numbers anyhow, were hung, focused and set the afternoon before the first dress rehearsal.

The director's hat however, was not the only one I wore. I also wore the producer's hat, serving as comptroller, meaning I had to manage the money. Getting the money into the bank, paying the bills, and overseeing every phase of activity to get the show on the stage, I soon learned more fully than I dreamed of during my Carnegie Tech days, how demanding the theater could be. I came to realize that of all the professions the theater is the most unrelenting in its demands. In the theater, nothing, but nothing, is allowed to interfere with getting "on with the show". The set and lights have to be ready for the opening night curtain, and the actors must be ready with their lines, gestures, movements, and in their places, in costume and make-up every night, with no liberty to suffer any indisposition, however minor. Sure, there's the possibility, in extremis, of an understudy, but not in our small grass roots operation, nor in most other theaters, except, on occasion, on Broadway.

As producer and stage director, I was obliged to accept the function of business manager as well, which meant it was my job to order the printed tickets and distribute them to the several points of sale. It was my job to write the press releases, send them on to the newspapers, compose our mailing pieces and program text, with typography and design by Suzanna whose many gifts, thank the Gods, included typographical design. A few days before that opening night of "Comedy of Errors," the husband of one of our seamstresses agreed to take over the House Manager's duties, and I was free to be nervous and exhilarated back stage on opening night, encouraging everyone, dashing back and forth to the front of the house to see that everything was in order, and that the arriving audience were getting their programs and were being seated properly. I insisted on reserved seats.

We did have a stage manager, who saw to it that each member of the cast was ready for his entrance, the props were ready for the actors, the lighting person (in this case, the lighting woman: Mary Lou was her name), was ready. What a relief when the moment came to open the doors to the public and to send Suzanna out in costume, to sit on the edge of the stage and start playing our overture, a medley of Elizabethan airs, on her recorder-flute..

That first season we managed with some mixed success to stage three plays at the Berkeley High Little Theater. Every production, indeed, every performance, spurred me on with greater urgency to find a theater space we could call our own. I was ready for any kind of space, ready for any kind of necessary transformation.

I remembered that during our year in Paris we had seen some small theater companies performing in odd spaces. Most of their buildings had been garages for auto mechanics. In 1951, the year we started, Off-Broadway had barely begun, and the concept of transforming a building like a warehouse, a restaurant, a retail store, or a parking lot into a performance space had not yet taken hold of our emerging grass roots theater movement, so there weren't many to inspire us. At one point, I decided to focus spe-cifically on finding a commercial garage, and signed up with three or four real estate agencies, looking for what would become our new theater.

In my eagerness to move into a place of our own, I simply ignored the question of how to pay the rent, get Pacific Telephone to give us a few lines, open an account with Pacific Gas and Electric, and Berkeley Water Works. Our ticket income was all the money we had, and by the third production I had learned to manage our finances so that, with box office receipts, I could pay for outstanding invoices after the first week-end, and keep some of our funds to take care of expenses incurred for the upcoming production. The whole process made Suzanna very ner-vous, and I could feel Helen's concern when she asked me, in the most studied casual way, how we were doing with our money. I guess I was living in a fool's paradise since I don't recall experiencing much anxiety, as justified as it might have been. As for the new playhouse which existed only in my dreams, those ongoing and everlasting dreams, I kept on a never ending look out and felt sure we could find the money, once we found the property.

Our first season at the Berkeley Little Theater at Berkeley High continued after "Comedy of Errors" with a lesser known Chekhov called "Ivanov" which was enjoying some success off- Broadway that season. We ended with "The Skin of Our Teeth" by Thornton Wilder. I was rehearsing the play when I learned that Wilder had graduated from Berkeley High before going East to Yale to start up his career, first with a number of one-act plays and then on to his historic success with "Our Town" on Broadway. I took that news to be a good omen for us, and it was.

As we rolled up our sleeves and got our second season on its way, I found teaching Subject A (sub-Freshman English) at the University of California Berkeley was a very rewarding experience for me. All my life I have loved teaching and, the interaction with students has always been for me a source of energy. The course, as I recall was based on a very stimulating number of texts, ranging from psychology to philosophy and history, all woven together by their common subject, "The Human Condition," The teaching salary was much better than the pay for collecting fares on the F Train to San Francisco. It didn't take long to realize that 12 hours of teaching per week, especially if I could arrange for a morning schedule, would be a fine way to have a steady income, and support us in making our dream come true. It also gave me at least half a day or more and every evening to serve the various needs of the Golden Hind.

When I accepted the Fulbright Grant for Europe in October of 1950, I withdrew from Carnegie Tech assuming I would be back the following year for the second year's work required for a Master's Degree. A year of European theater, plus the joy of sharing life and visions of our own theater with Suzanna, changed all that. The University of

California Berkeley. did not offer a Master's in Theater at that time, but Mills College in Oakland, a distinguished college did, and my application was accepted.. I learned that though Mills was a women's college, it welcomed men in the graduate programs in the arts, - theater, music, dance and fine arts. In fact I looked in vain for other men on campus as I wandered from library to theater to classes. However I did notice one other male student always coming and going to and from the Music Building. Our paths hardly ever crossed, but I learned that he was indeed, Dave Brubeck, the young jazz star, already embarked on his notable career. In fact he was studying composition with Darius Milhaud, the renown French symphonic composer who lived in Paris and came every other year to teach in residence to a small handful of students at Mills. (That explained to me a year or two later, how the Milhauds, whom I knew to be Parisians, came to our Golden Hind theater from time to time , as I will briefly note as this account goes on.).

The Mills Registrar determined that my credits for my course work at Carnegie Tech were all acceptable to add to the work I planned at Mills, and a Master's could be mine with only one year's work at Mills!

The theater faculty at Mills was not large, but especially inviting to me because I recognized the name, Arch Lauterer, on the faculty and I knew him to be a respected stage designer in New York, especially noted for his stage designs for Martha Graham. After an interview it was clear we shared many of the same prejudices, or visions, for the contemporary theater. He was clearly another American designer inspired by Gordon Craig, and the anti-realists. Needless to say we got on famously, and I was granted a Master's Degree in Fine Arts in Theater at the end of my year's work, which included research, design, theater history, and production. In fact the resources of the department were somewhat limited, and Arch agreed to accept my Golden Hind production of "The Knight of the Burning Pestle" at the end of our second season, as fulfillment of one of my requirements. He raved about our production, because he clearly saw how much we were in accord on the design and use of the stage space. The MFA came in good stead all through the rest of my theater career, clearing the way to appointments which we sorely needed, a welcome source of steady income to support life and limb through the years. Our grass roots theater did indeed take root, but we were a long time in growing enough to provide a living wage. No matter. The fulfillment in bringing the Golden Hind to life and the joy in teaching actually nourished each other.

The second season started with Shakespeare's "Measure for Measure". The production which followed "Measure" would play in December just before the Christmas recess. We chose "The Knight of the Burning Pestle", a raucous comedy by Beaumont and Fletcher, contemporaries of Shakespeare. It's the story of a greengrocer and his wife who take their apprentice to the theater for his very first time. He is completely taken in by what's happening on stage and believes the actors are real people in real distress. He jumps up onto the set and takes over as the brave knight who protects the ingénue from what he believes to be real dangers threatening her. Written in 1607, it may well be the first theater piece that started a tradition in theater plots where a member of the audience loses his sense of reality and runs up on stage to tangle with the villain to save the ingénue threatened with a fate worse than death.

It was during our second season that the San Francisco critics began to drive over to Berkeley to review our shows. "The Knight of the Burning Pestle" was haled by Paine Kickerbocker of the **San Francisco Chronicle**. He wrote, "The Loveliest Night of the Year was 'The Knight of the Burning Pestle' at the Golden Hind," and for the next three or four years we always included in our season a handful of performances of "The Knight" early in December to start off the Christmas holidays.

By the time we were about to begin our third season, our lucky stars began to shine. On day in Spring I had a call from a local real estate office that there was a small building for rent on San Pablo Avenue in Berkeley, rather close to the Bay, and not too far from the university campus.

I grabbed Suzanna by the hand and jumped into our little sports car, and eagerly drove the five minutes to 1505 San Pablo Avenue. There, in the middle of the block about ten feet back from the curb, was a modest building about 50 x 100 feet, with glass windows on the front, and parking space between the building and the sidewalk sufficient for any delivery trucks which the original owner might have expected to need parking space. It was an empty building ready to undergo a transformation. Built to be an industrial laundry, it could lend itself to conversion into a commercial garage, or better yet, to an innovative theater space for the Company of the Golden Hind.

The real estate agent told us the building, completed a few years earlier, had never seen operations as the owner had intended as a commercial laundry. The deal had never gone through, so the owners were eager to get some rent out of the property so long as it would be rented "as is". We saw at first sight it would suit us to a T!

In negotiating the lease, I asked the landlord at the signing to agree to let us have the building rent free for the first 60 days. She was eager to sign and ready and willing to accept our terms.

Driving home for a drink to celebrate after signing the lease, I said to Suzanna, "I've been trying to dream up a name for our new theater. And guess what's come to me?"

"Well, I'm not surprised. You with your dreams. Tell me," she said.

"I think we should call it The Golden Hind Playbox. What do you think? Then as we grow and move into something bigger, we'll call our next space The Golden Hind Playhouse. After that, the next building will be our Golden Hind Theater. How's that?"

"I love it," she said without pause or hesitation.

We were relieved to see the building had two functioning bathrooms near the front, and one in the rear, so that we conformed to city statutes on sanitary requirements. The entire floor space was clean, smooth, poured concrete, and there was an arched wooden roof, with exposed 2 x 4 beams, skylights for daylight, and lots of electrical outlets to facilitate our theatrical lighting. In short it was perfect for us and ready for our transformation with no need for a local Frank Lloyd Wright. We took the measurements home and easily roughed out a floor plan. We agreed from the start that we wanted an "open stage", a stage without a curtain, without a proscenium. For us it also meant a stage that evolved organically, out of the architecture of the building. With the words of Thornton Wilder so critical of the middle class domestic interior in mind, we had no intention of creating a true-to-life realistic setting in any of our productions, even when we might stage a play set in a living or sitting or bedroom. First, we planned to place an interior wall cutting off ten feet at the back of the building to separate the acting space from the backstage with its common dressing room, make-up tables, restroom, and very limited storage. Then we decided on another interior wall at the front of the building to create a lobby with box-office to the side, and access to the two restrooms required by the sanitary code. We decided to keep the front windows clear to show the inside lobby and to hold posters about our current season.

The interior theater space was more challenging. We had Leonard Brown (Brownie), our genius technical director, build three levels of platforms to hold audience seating, and they were installed on two adjoining sides of the interior space, with the acting area back in the corner opposite the audience. Our stage was a triangular platform raised ten inches above the concrete floor, with the apex of the triangle fitting into the corner opposite the seating. We were able to build a kind of crows nest up near the roof, above the heads of the seated audience. This was where we had our lighting console, with a limited number of electronic dimmers easily mounted on a desk Brownie built for the purpose. Only a few years earlier, Yale Professor of Lighting George Izenour, had invented a light weight, flexible and completely revolutionary system for dimming the lights. He found a way to team up a number of what were essentially small vacuum tubes, replacing the traditional cumbersome iron "resistance dimmer" that weighed hundreds of pounds and was usually installed in rows attached to the wall at the rear of the building, back stage where the lighting technicians could not see the stage and had to rely on their ears to hear the dialog onstage or on the stage manager who whispered the cues to them.

I was delighted to have our lighting technicians in front of the stage so they could see and hear perfectly.

Once we had our floor plan sketched out on graph paper, we went to work, keeping in mind we had only 8 weeks before we would have to start paying rent. For construction of those separating sheetrock walls, we found a wonderfully warm and good-humored carpenter. Antonio was a Sicilian immigrant with his own contractor's license and a very willing heart, and with good friends in the Berkeley Building Department whom he could easily dissuade from inspecting our workmanship too rigorously. Something like 50 years old, he was happy to be the foreman of our construction crew of young actors and friends and to guide us in following his instructions every inch of the way. He brought in his own scaffolding and ladders, and he spent long days with us, always in good cheer, until the would-be laundry was miraculously transformed into a could-be theater. We needed those eight weeks, for our volunteer crew to get the job done. We needed all the weekends plus week-day afternoons and evenings to make it possible.

Antonio was a treasure, and we could see after only one week that we would meet our deadline and were confident we would have box-office receipts to pay the rent. There were two really daunting challenges still to face. We had to install seating for the audience, and we had to decide on what color to paint the theater interior.

Soon after we started the construction project, Helen came up from Long Beach on one of her usual visits to give us the support we needed, including, as I recall, some recent unexpected "small dividends" from Harry's oil investments.

When it came to the interior color, Helen had her ideas.

"Rachmael," she said, "I remember seeing Isadora Duncan dance on a bare stage, when she came to Wichita when I was a girl. You know she never used any stage settings, always danced in front of a lovely deep blue curtain. I really wish you would consider painting all our interior walls a rich, dark blue, Isadora's blue, especially since we don't have any curtains, front or back. It'll make all the actors and their costumes look beautiful. You'll see. What do you think?"

At first it seemed to me it would be less than gracious if I didn't consider looking at some paint samples with Helen before making any decisions.

"Helen," I said, "I'm off to Kelly–Moore for paint samples and you'll tell us which shades of blue come closest to Isadora's blue."

I found Isadora's blue. Helen was so right. The blue went on, and Helen gleefully spoke up, "You see," she said in her stage soprano voice, "I told you so. You told me Isadora lived here in Berkeley for a time. Maybe it was Isadora's ghost that brought her blue to my mind."

We all took a hand in painting the hundreds of square feet of sheetrock walls. We did three coats to have it right and get Helen's final approval. She asked me how much one gallon of paint cost, and had me tell her how many gallons I had bought, and on the spot wrote me a check for all of them. The blue was perfect on our walls, neither too dark and ominous, nor too vibrant and bright. It was perfect as a background for our actors, for Suzanna's costumes and our lighting. From then on we called it "Helen's Blue". By then we were all working hard seven days a week, morning, noon, and night transforming the laundry. There was a Doggie Diner a few blocks away on San Pablo Avenue, and Helen always knew when to send one of us out with a handful of cash to come back with hotdogs, hamburgers and French fries to keep everyone working into the night.

After two grueling weeks of work, work, work, Helen ruled that we must take Sunday afternoon off. No argument from me. "... and don't go calling me a battle-axe on this account, Rachmael," she said with a laugh. I agreed without hesitation.

Sunday came, and around midday Helen spoke up, "Rachmael, you know it's always been on my mind that you said Isadora actually lived and taught here in the Berkeley hills. You think we could find her house? Wouldn't you love to see it?"

I said, "Sure. Let's try."

In fact, I did find the house, or what was left of it after a disastrous fire there around 1918. From the panoramic road going up into the Berkeley Hills we saw the Grecian columns she had had designed for her school and residence. Then we found the driveway with its forbidding sign marked "Private". Helen urged me to just put the nose of the car into the driveway. As I did so, an older woman came out, in thong fitted sandals, flowing blond hair, wispy sarong kind of dress, and an absolutely beatific smile. "Can I help you?" she asked, as if we didn't know we were trespassing.

Helen piped up quickly. "Forgive us for intruding, but you know I saw Isadora dance when I was a girl in Kansas, and I understand she lived near here. I'm dying to see her house, even if it's just from the roadside. Are we anywhere close?"

"Indeed you are." said our lovely lady, laughing. "This," she pointed to the house behind her, "this was Isadora's house and where she taught her modern dancing. You can see the Grecian columns that survived the fire that destroyed most of the house. She restored some columns, and then just built rooms among the ruins, and went on here with her dance classes for several years. I live here now. I'm a member of the family, the family that has survived all those wonderful years. You know her brother, Augustus Duncan lived here for many years before going off to Paris where he lived out his life.

"Won't you come in? I'd love for you to see some of the house."

We thanked her for her hospitality, and we enjoyed the visit. Well, Helen always invited unanticipated pleasures.

Construction continued with the paint crew following closely behind. The cost of the bleacher platforms for the seats we had not yet found was in our budget and were under construction by Brownie. I charged the lumber to our account at Truitt and White Lumber, a few blocks from us toward the water front. The next formidable problem was to find seating, and I did not want 162 folding chairs like those you'd find in a church basement. I was determined. I knew of Cleveland Wrecking on the Bay in nearby Richmond, where useable building parts, furniture and fixtures from every demolished building in the Bay Area finally ended up and became available on the cheap to be put to creative use by any ready buyer.

Hoping against hope, I went down to the salvage yards and asked if they ever had used theater seats to sell, that we could afford. No, they told me, but there was a company that specialized in salvaging materials from old movie houses. They were in Pleasanton, a nearby community, and might have something that would serve us. I called the company and, sure enough, they had just closed down an old movie house in one of those small East Bay towns, Danville, I think. I could have a few hundred of the old seats at $1.50 a piece as-is, but they were still screwed to each other and to the floor of the old movie house, and we'd have to unscrew them and move them out ourselves. Some were banged up and useless, but we could choose the best 180 seats I could find and, of course, we'd have to haul them away in our own truck.

I drove out to see them the following day, and they were pretty horrible. Suzanna was appalled. But, at $1.50 apiece, I could even write a check then and there for them and pick them up pronto. I arranged to pick up the seats early on the following Saturday morning when I knew our whole volunteer crew of men and women could show up at 1505 San Pablo Avenue and get those chairs ready for our expected distinguished audience.

I arranged to rent a big flatbed truck which we decided would do the job in two trips. I appointed myself as the truck driver so I could, for the first time in my life, drive a flatbed truck. The rental people taught me about "double clutching" and other details for safe handling of a big flatbed. I learned things about truck driving that were never taught at Carnegie Tech. It was unforgettable, and a thrilling experience to have all that power under my control! In later seasons when we did some one night stands in schools and gymnasiums around the Bay, I was always the self-appointed, self-satisfied, grinning, lucky guy who drove the flatbed truck carrying the sets and costumes.

Meanwhile, back at the Playbox, the theater seats were unloaded and we were overwhelmed by a massive bout of group giggling when we saw the full depth of the dirt, the grime, the spilled coke, the chewing gum under the seats, and the broken springs. First, we cleaned them up, got rid of those beyond repair, and replaced some of the leatherette seat covering. Brownie saw how to attach them in rows, and screw them down onto the bleacher platforms he had built for that purpose.

As you walked into the theater, it was the unattractive back of each seat that caught your eye and it was clear we had to do something about this eyesore. New backs were out of the question, of course, requiring much too much money and work. But happily I remembered the slipcovers covering the backs of outdoor cafe chairs in Paris during the summer months of our Fulbright year. Why not stitch up covers for the backs of our "new" theater seats, with ties stitched to the bottom of each cover to keep them from slipping off? Slipcovers had the further advantage of being removable so we could get them laundered periodically without too much trouble.

While most of the crew were working with scouring powder, bleach, paint scrapers, and large quantities of steel wool in attacking all the grunge that had to be removed, we had two or three sewing machines working away with seamstresses cutting up and sewing together the seat back covers. We had measured the backs the week before, and bought from Sears Roebuck their inexpensive blue denim in a shade of washed blue harmonious with Helen's Blue on the surrounding walls.

All day, into the evening, the beer flowed, the pizzas and hot dogs were devoured, cokes were poured, and the Doggie Diner donuts were our dessert. A good time was had by all. Helen commented that it felt like her Presbyterian Church Suppers back in her days in Kansas, or maybe an odd sort of sewing bee.

There was a pole, about the height of a street light, right in the middle of our parking space in front of our building, and Brownie was able to mount a wooden sign at the top, and I had had the sign painter's shop in town paint a sturdy wooden sign for us. Then Brownie got way up on the pole, nailed up the sign, and hooked it up with electricity so we could have the sign lit up every evening as we wished. It proudly proclaimed, **The Golden Hind Playbox**.

As I had decided, there was to be no proscenium, not even a suggestion of one, nor any other construction, so that the actors and the audience shared together one large space with no line of separation between them.

For opening night I chose to revive a play by Anouilh we had done two seasons earlier at the Berkeley Little Theater with success at the box office as well as on stage. The French title is "L'Invitation au Chateau" (Invitation to the Chateau). But in the Christopher Fry English adaptation it's called "Ring Round the Moon" . A charming play, it was not particularly difficult to restage and it seemed a good choice for offering a jolly evening, witty and wise, for our opening performances.

We freshened the costumes, repainted the set, which was a collection of set pieces, including decorative panels, draperies, and interesting turn-of-the-century looking furnishings. At the first Playbox performance, I made my usual welcoming remarks as I had at the Berkeley Little Theater. Here in our own house I could also invite them all to our newly decorated lobby to share a glass of champagne and some *petit fours* after the opening night performance. It was thrilling, lovely, joyous, a celebration!. Indeed, it was our dream coming true. Over my shoulder I could sense the presence of Hallie Flanagan, Gordon Craig, and Lee Strasberg.

The curving stage, and the wood structure with the arched timbered ceiling with Helens Blue on the walls all created a harmonious housing for our kind of theater. We had found our "habitation and a name," to borrow from Shakespeare's "Dream".

The audiences as well as the critics from San Francisco were receptive, even enthusiastic. During our fourth weekend I noted that on Saturday night we had a distinguished Parisian couple in the audience. The world renowned composer, Darius Milhaud in residence at Mills College and Madeleine, his actress wife, had called to reserve tickets and I made a mental note of it when I saw his name on our reservation sheet. I had some qualms about his being in the house because I had chosen for incidental music, his suite, "Le Boeuf Sous le Toit" written in the '20's. The title is the name of a scandalously famous bar still running in Paris and dating back to the 20's, and the music fit very well with the whiff of the 20's in our set and costumes.

At the intermission I went out to greet the Milhauds and to say how honored and pleased we were to have them in our Playbox. We shook hands, and they told me how much they admired our new home. Then Mme Milhaud looked me straight in the eye, and said "But, Monsieur, isn't that his music?" pointing to her husband.

For an instant I shuddered, since I knew quite well we had not asked for permission nor paid royalties for the use of the music on our audio tape.

"Yes, Madame," I said. "I've taken the liberty of playing 'Le Boeuf Sous le Toit.' I hope you don't mind?"

She turned to him." Idiot!" she said with a smile. Then to me, "I told him it's his music. But he remembers nothing. I couldn't remember the name myself. You see we are enjoying the play, immensely."

IV - MENTORS AND METAPHORS

It was inevitable as time went on that some members of the audience would catch on to the fact that our productions had, as they put it, "a style of their own". Our programs announced that the repertoire selected for each season was planned to include one work by Shakespeare, one from the later 18th century, (i.e.- Goldsmith's "She Stoops to Conquer"), one or two from the 19th and early 20th century (i.e. Oscar Wilde, Bernard Shaw) and one contemporary, (i.e.- Tennessee Williams, Sean O'Casey, Arthur Miller). During the summer months, to give those in the regular roster of actors who wanted it some breathing space, I always planned a musical production, - a chamber production of Mozart or Bernstein, for example. Guided by commitment to balance and variety, we selected plays following this plan.

Season after season, we remained true to our commitment to a choice of plays that celebrate the human condition. Occasionally a member of the audience would comment on our repertoire, indicating that they caught on to our purpose in always being true to our intention ... "to stage plays that celebrate the human condition, plays where the human spirit achieves affirmation, exaltation, even redemption". When I did receive comments that we were "not like the others" the comment was, thankfully, usually intended as a compliment. I interpreted these remarks to refer to our productions, to our unique visualization of the play, not to the plays themselves. To my mind the comment was evoked by our holding to stage worthy, dramatic theatrical styles that suited the play.. When one audience member said to me, "But Mr. ben-Avram, all your plays are so stylized; you always show us characters that are believable but they're not really like the true-to-life men and women we see around us. Your sets are always imaginative and interesting, but we never see a stage set looking like the actual living room we live in. That's why I say you're always so imaginative, but always so stylized."

"Yes," I replied, "without doubt we are that. But let me remind you, if you've seen more than a few of our productions, that the so-called stylization you recognize originates in the play itself, and that explains why it's apparent that no two plays are produced by us with the same style. In fact, there's a down side to this approach to production style and design, because it means that we can never use the same costumes and set pieces from one production to the next. It means a huge rental check each month to pay for storage space for our stock of costumes and sets."

These conversations invariably ended with, "Oh, I hope you understand we love your productions; we always enjoy your theater. You're so different."

To which I always replied, more or less, "How good of you to say so. I'm always glad to hear it."

After several seasons in Berkeley, one of our "regulars", Mrs. Hopkins, cornered me at the end of a performance she had enjoyed of a play by Anouilh.. "Rachmael," she said, "what is your secret? [I'm paraphrasing here.] What makes your productions so different from the others we go to see? We always come away from a Golden Hind show in such a good mood, even when the play is a serious drama, even when it doesn't have a happy ending.

"Everyone in your company acts with so much energy, they all speak up so well and so clearly, they all have so much verve. You make them move so easily around the stage, as if you had choreographed them. I certainly noticed it in your 'Cosi'. It seemed as if they were dancing to the music as well as singing it. It was sparkling. So tell me, what is your secret?"

Of course I knew what she meant, what she was driving at, and I did my best to be clear and brief. In fact Suzanna and I had discussed from the start our Golden Hind approach to theater production. I went on with our conversation, doing the best I could to describe for Mrs. Hopkins, our dramatic intentions, hoping to avoid sounding stuffy or self righteous. I told her we were inspired by some notable mentors. I spoke of Hallie Flanagan, of course, and Gordon Craig, Thornton Wilder, and the lesser known Professor Francis Fergusson, who all wrote on the art of the theater. I went on to add a number of pioneering set designers, especially Robert Edmond Jones, Lee

Simonson, Donald Oenslager, and Boris Aronson who had inspired us. What they had in common was a rejection of what we recognize as realism, or verisimilitude. They made no attempt to create "the spitting image" of life. These mentors, whom we knew only from their work, concurred with Oscar Wilde's dictum, "In matters of importance, style, not sincerity is the thing." A large part of our current theater world, including all of the 20th century until today, unfortunately still believes that sincerity is the thing, the only thing.

What Mrs Hopkins and our other critics, professional and otherwise, needed to keep in mind was the wise observations of Thornton Wilder. His plays are acknowledged American classics, but he also wrote essays on the theater. Speaking as a leading light of the Broadway theater, he wrote that the theater is "the greatest of all the arts." But he deplored the fact that the 19th century went in for realistic domestic interiors and realistic props on the stage, thereby reducing the theater, in his very own words, "to a minor art and an inconsequential diversion." I quote Jeremy McCarter, theater critic at **New York Magazine,** who, in a recent review of a new edition of Wilder's plays put it best when he wrote that Wilder called for the need

> ... to abandon naturalism and rediscover the tools of Shakespeare and the Greeks: stage conventions that convey - a marvelous distinction - 'not verisimilitude, but reality.'"

In Wilder's essays he echoes Gordon Craig's point of view, in reference to realism on the stage.

In the 1920's Craig was ridiculed in London when he trumpeted his revolutionary views stating that he despised the 19ᵗʰ century's stage attempt at verisimilitude. In "The Theater Advancing" , which Suzanna and I took as a gospel of the theater, he wrote:

> Doubtless the cross on which the Saviour was crucified was an ordinary and rough wooden structure, but when it reaches the cathedral it becomes a precious work of art, in no way realistic. ... Why do they (who build cathedrals) make this transformation? Because it (the true cross) is too good a thing ever to be imitated; because it would be said they were pretending to put up the real cross; but every one realizes this (cross of gold) is in relation to an object made holy by thought. We fashion symbolic crosses, trees, standing for the real thing, made in precious metals. In other words we look to exalt the experience of the cross shown on the altar, by the use of precious metals.

In New York, Jones, in his book **The Dramatic Imagination,** addressed young aspiring stage directors and scene designers, standing up for all that he learned from Gordon Craig. He succinctly states: "I mean that even when you're at the top of the ladder precariously hanging the stage lights, I would have you keep in your souls some images of magnificence."

In the 1950's there was no professional association of theater people sworn to free the theater of verisimilitude or we would have been charter members. But indeed, we were fanatic converts, inspired by Jones's urge to magnificence and we followed his dictum religiously. We looked for plays where our "images of magnificence" would fit. Following Wilder's lead, I looked for and found plays that captured our imagination by their mythical inner life. That meant avoiding most of our contemporary playwrights whom Wilder criticized for their "childish attempts to be 'real'". This avoidance would include earlier plays set down in a later era such as O'Neill 's "Mourning Becomes Electra", which, though based on the mythical Greek "Oresteia", becomes merely a domestic melodrama. In the end, it fails to exalt its characters to their heroic potential. A play with a mythical inner life is a play in which a character comes to life in the grip of his demon, his shadow, that attribute with which he was born into this world, as we all were. Among the many plays that come to mind besides Wilder's "Our Town", "Skin of Our Teeth" and "The Matchmaker," is Synge's early 20th century "Playboy of the Western World".

In the kind of play that spoke to our Golden Hind vision, the main character is a personification of the archetype, a mythical creature, explored so fully by Carl Jung.

In serious drama or tragedy, to paraphrase Francis Fergusson's "tragic rhythm" in his profound book, **The Idea of a Theater**, the demon-driven hero, through suffering, grows in consciousness, "mindfulness" we could say, and becomes more fully aware of his person-hood as he passes from the purpose that propels him, through the passion that he suffers as a consequence, to a new perception or awakening.

In comedy the protagonist usually opposes the culture's social status quo, is compelled to transform it, and, for his pains, wins his rightful prize, the girl with the golden hair. To sum up, the Company of the Golden Hind presented plays that showed the deeper reality of the human dilemma rather than our mere daily challenges.

It seemed to me that our Mrs. Hopkins rather easily accepted my remarks. I decided that if she could connect with this description of "where we were coming from" (to echo my students' vernacular), I could go on and get to the meat of the matter, which is what we called "the dramatic metaphor."

"Mrs. Hopkins," I said, "I appreciate knowing how truly interested you are in our creative process, so before we complete this conversation, I want to explain our particular production planning process.

I went on to explain that what the viewer may think is a secret way of looking at the stage is no secret at all. Once we agree on the play, and agree on an interpretation based on the ideas I've just described, we start to work on the production. First we get aligned on the interpretation of the play, the meaning that moves the plot and the characters. Then we go on to think about the staging,-- the acting, the sets, costumes, lighting, and all the other technical aspects of production. Our approach to any play is to delve into the meaning of the text and to explore our own imagination, looking for what we call a 'dramatic metaphor'.

A metaphor, I explained, is a figure of speech, in which a comparison is made between two seemingly dissimilar things, or two concepts, and a word is used to describe or refer to one thing which is usually used when referring to the other . Here's an example; - The President hit *a home run* with the budget he presented to the Congress. 'Home run' is the metaphor. It is what champion baseball players hit, not presidents. Running the country is not exactly the same as playing a game of baseball. But that can be a good way to describe more vividly a particular political success. The example is typical of the way metaphor is used for dynamic emphasis.

"Yes, I see," she said. "We use that kind of metaphor all the time, even without thinking about it. But what in the world is a dramatic metaphor as you use the term?"

I scratched my head a bit. "Maybe you'll forgive me for quoting Shakespeare. In 'As You Like It' he has a character say,

All the world's a stage,

And all the men and women merely players;

His metaphor compares the artifice of the stage, or the theater, to the daily reality in the world. It brings into play the concept of "as if".. It brings us to view what's happening in a play, "as if" it were true to life, and at the same time reminds us of the underlying archetypes, the cultural myths, the heroes caught in the grip of the human condition."

I went on to explain that, at the Golden Hind, we like to create an appropriate dynamic in dramatizing the events in the play, and we want the characters our actors create for you to be larger than life. I reminded her that the theater expects the audience to agree to "the willing suspension of disbelief" for the brief few hours you're in the theater. Over all, at the Golden Hind, we want you to enjoy the total dramatic experience, -- the dialogue, the acting, the decor, the costumes. Beyond that, we want to move you emotionally. When you go to see an exhibition of Rembrandt or Picasso, you recognize that the portrait you're looking at represents a real person. But you know very well it's not the person; it's a representation of a person. With Picasso, it's even a distortion of what the real person or object looks like, but you see through the artist's eyes, and that's what makes the painting come to life and give you pleasure. There's a lovely joke in modern art history that serves us here. Magritte, the modern artist has a famous painting of an apple, a beautiful green apple. He has given the painting a title,- "This Is Not An Apple" *(C'est n'est pas une Pomme)*. Well, we see the stage as a metaphor for something real or imagined, but the Hamlet on stage is not really Hamlet, and the stage décor identified as Ellsinore Castle in Denmark, is not really Ellsinore. He is an actor named Bill, and the theater is a building on San Pablo Avenue in Berkeley. The play takes place every night, not in Denmark but in that theater.

I continued to explain that we at the Golden Hind believe that realism in the theater, where the actors walk and talk and look like themselves in real life, is not as interesting as when the actors, as collaborators with the audience, themselves, metaphorically. They are metaphors for the characters they impersonate. And we work to create a stage decor, costumes, lighting and a whole production, to manifest the characters, and so become elements in a work of art. We want you to enjoy the music, the language, the acting, the stage scene itself as part of that work of art, because they are all elements, all part of the metaphor that expresses the meaning of the play and contributes to your enjoyment of it all.

"Rachmael," she said, "I'm beginning to catch on. I guess we're all accustomed to looking at the stage and expecting it to be just like the real world. Really natural, if you know what I mean."

"Mrs. Hopkins, I know just what you mean," I replied. "And I thank you for your interest in our work."

She smiled and had a question. "But, you know, I'm wondering about your actors. They all speak and move with such vitality, call it energy, maybe verve. What makes them so different on your stage from the actors we see all around us here at the other resident theaters? Do you pump them up with strong coffee before the lights go up on the play? What do you do to them to make them stand out so much?"

"Mrs. Hopkins, that's a really good question, and I've already answered it in part. You see, when we fix on the dramatic metaphor for a production, we have to imagine the characters in such a way that harmonizes with the dramatic metaphor we've chosen. For example, when the metaphor is the circus, the actors have to act like clowns.

Our intention is that they come across with all the energy we enjoy when we see clowns jumping around, making us laugh, exaggerating their movements and their speech."

I went on to explain that the one principle we follow in every production is to suit the speech to the character's action and manners, his station in life. Just as Hamlet said, speaking to his Players when they arrived at Ellsinore.

> Speak the speech, I pray you, as I pronounced it to you -- tripping on the tongue; but if you mouth it as so many of your players do, I had as leif the town crier spoke my lines. Nor do not saw the air too much, with your hand thus, but use all gently; for the very torrent, tempest, and as I may say, the whirlwind of your passion, you must acquire and beget a temperance that may give it smoothness.

Nowadays so many actors, trained to be emotionally sincere, avoid "mouthing" and try to speak as naturally as they can, to avoid seeming affected, artificial. But, to my mind, the actor must always be interesting as well as sincere. So if he's consumed by passion, we want to hear it as he speaks the speech; we want him to create onstage a true semblance of that passion with temperance and smoothness. A trained actor learns how to unlock a part of his own psyche that reveals his character's passions. Unfortunately we often see characters submitting to the limitations that are the limitations in the actor's own life. It is true, of course, there are some characters, as in Chekhov, for example, who live with their deepest feelings bottled up. In such a case, the acting problem is to find a way to suggest what's bottled up, what's repressed, without the actor falling into the trap of showing us his own repressed self on stage. In speech and gesture he must always communicate even to the last row of the theater.

I explained that I understood that when Oscar Wilde said, "In matters of importance, style not sincerity is the thing," he assumed that sincerity is a given, a fundamental foundation for every artistic expression. However, without the dynamics of style, including manner, 'temperance with smoothness', the sincerity with which the actor projects his character soon becomes boring. When Gertrude Stein proclaims that "the function of the artist is to be exciting," we agree, but we think that doesn't mean we should give up authenticity.

At the Golden Hind, I explained, we work in rehearsal to evoke the character and to project it's personality in the style or manner with which the character moves, sits, and talks. The thing I find unacceptable, is to see a performance where the actors are all being very sincere and authentic on stage, but just being themselves, and little more. It's not enough, I say (I have even been known to shout it in rehearsal). We may be able to believe what they say, in the way they relate to each other with anger, love, hatred, lust, but we can't hear them beyond the third row. We sometimes get the feeling we are eavesdropping. What a bore! We tell the actors at the Golden Hind to "Act Up", not "Act Down". How to do that is the actors' trade. Without that training and skill, he becomes just another real-life but ordinary person.

Trying to moderate my self-assurance in this matter I spoke up, "Acting is an art and involves training and technique. Maybe you'd like to come to a rehearsal sometime and see how our actors do their work, apply their skill to making the characters come to life with both sincerity and style. The acting in Shakespeare must be sufficiently passionate so that we believe Hamlet, the character, when he says 'Oh, what a rogue and peasant slave am I.' We need to believe in Juliet's passion when it moves her to say, 'O, Romeo.... be but sworn my love, And I'll no longer be a Capulet.' In a more contemporary situation like 'The Death of a Salesman', the actress playing Willie Loman's wife must show us a woman in pain who speaks from the heart when she says to her two sons, about her failing husband, 'Attention must be paid.' Shakespeare, has been hypnotizing audiences for several hundred years, not with his realistic conversation, but with his exalted poetic language.

I noted she had spoken about sparkle, which reminded me of stage spectacle in all its aspects,- actors, sets, costume, lighting. We believe that the spectacle only prepares the stage for the real magic which comes from the actor. The magic is there because the actor has wound himself up to make us believe that, in impersonating the character of Hamlet, for instance, he feels the loss of his father sufficiently to pursue the murderer and speak with the passion the playwright assigns to him. It is the actor himself who is a metaphor for the Prince and we willingly suspend our disbelief so we can believe in his grief as he expresses it with Shakespeare's moving language. We do the same for the actor who plays Lear when he shows us the king's rage. At the end, we also see his humanity which comes to light as a result of his suffering. But the actor is not suffering. He is having a grand time, enjoying his work. He loves it. He convinces us to believe in the King's anger, sorrow and final transformation. It is the King who is transformed, not the actual person who takes on the role of the King.

I concluded, "Now you know our secret. It's not really a magician's trick, the dramatic metaphor, but it may end up being magical."

I thought I was getting perilously close to sounding ponderous, so I hurriedly gave her a few examples of dramatic metaphor as it applied to actual productions. First, I spoke about how we interpreted the "Comedy of Errors" to be about twin brothers who wake up to realize we are all brothers if we only knew it. The metaphor was drawn from the world of circus. The stage setting was a theatrical , not a real, circus tent, the costumes were variations on clown costumes, the make-up was definitely variations on clown white-face, and the staging included a lot of what could be called zany clowning around. The theme of the comedy, as I said, is serious; the comedy, hilarious. I added quickly that in fact we were inspired by a wonderful painting called "Entering the Ring" by a 19th century French artist, Bombois. It shows a group of clowns about to enter a circus ring. The mood, the feeling, the spacing on the canvas, all taken together, suggested to me the dramatic metaphor which ended up serving our production of Shakespeare's comedy.

Later on, long after my conversation with Mrs. Hopkins, as our imagination expanded, we found metaphors in a growing variety of sources. For "King Lear," our metaphor was drawn from stone sculptures on 12th century English churches in East Anglia. Our cast of characters was made to look like the 12th century statues come to life in costumes molded out of heavily starched jute and velvet draperies, which Suzanna found at the Goodwill, all dyed by her capable hands to resemble the color of weathered stone.

In contrast, when we did the musical "The Boy Friend," a spoof of twenties musicals, the sets were intentionally garish, made to look like old fashioned corny vaudeville sets, with costumes that were cartoon exaggerations of the twenties. The dances, singing, and mannered speech, also cartoon-like to some degree, had the audiences falling out of their seats. The dramatic metaphor for "The Boy Friend" was the typical twenties musical pushed to an extreme.

Our production of Tennessee Williams's "Glass Menagerie" took a totally different approach to metaphor. We took our cue from the opening speech directed to the audience by the character, Tom. He tells us that this is his "memory play," a dream. So we picked up on that and made the play a kind of dream play. We had the whole set bathed in shades of blue light (there's a reference to blue roses in the script); we suggested in the lighting design that the stage was always bathed in moonlight. For the crucial dinner scene with the Gentleman Caller we warmed up the stage with the lighting and with the mother, Amanda's, treasured ball gown, to suit the mood and atmosphere the scene called for.

When we did Mozart's "Cosi fan Tutte", it was as if our singers were Meissen-ware china characters come to life, dancing on an Eighteenth Century music box.

At the end of my discussion of dramatic metaphor, I began to feel I had taken too much of Mrs. Hopkins' time, though she remained politely attentive through it all. As I completed my explanation, she thanked me and said she was looking forward to our next offering.

When I got home that evening and reported my conversation to Suzanna, we talked about our use of dramatic metaphor and realized anew that we had both been happily and successfully mesmerized by our mentors. Having grown up in New York, my experience of theater was the greater, but Suzanna easily shared my anti-realism convictions. In truth, our productions were always a happy collaboration. As we sat talking over a glass of wine in our old Victorian house on Virginia Street in Berkeley, within walking distance to the Playbox, we were facing our framed copy of a famous photograph of Martha Graham, one of our idols. We saw her as one of the few truly great artists of the American theater, together with Wilder, Jones and the others I have mentioned earlier. Her work was one of the most important sources of our inspiration. Her dances were to my mind, mythic in conception, and her beautifully articulated metaphors always came from the depths of her own psyche. Graham taught us much that was new about how to integrate sets, costumes, lighting and the use of space in mapping out stage movement.

Another rich source of creativity for us was modern American musical comedy as well as modern dance. I do believe the musical play in America is certainly our most successful and most popular form of theater, and certainly musical productions all come to life as a result of the productions' use of dramatic metaphor. Scene design, costume, singing, staging, dancing, – all are hightened, carried out far beyond mere realistic representation. All the elements are larger than life, yet all are integrated into a unified artistic whole based on a dramatic metaphor.

My talk with Mrs. Hopkins made me more fully conscious of how much I owed to Gordon Craig's pervading influence. He wrote a whole shelf full of volumes on his vision of the theater's future. In his passion he declared that, for the theater to advance, it must leave behind the 19th century theater of realistic and naturalistic acting and design. Metaphor, metaphor, imaginative and illuminating metaphor, is what raises the theater up to the heights of its artistic potential and enriches our lives, as it is meant to do.

Of all the glowing words thrown like bouquets at us by the critics (and we had our share of tomatoes as well!), nothing gladdened our hearts so much as when we read in the **San Francisco Chronicle** that at the Company of the Golden Hind you were sure to enjoy an "evening of **wonder and delight**".

Knight of the Burning Pestle

Measure for Measure

Dybbuk

Dybbuk

Comedy of Errors

The Boy Friend

The Boy Friend

Ring Round the Moon

Abduction from the Seraglio

Barber of Seville

V - Our Time In "The Times"

Our seventh season at the Playbox, '57-'58 began without our having an inkling of how memorable it would be. Public response to our style of production grew in enthusiasm, and ticket sales encouraged us to give free rein to our creative intuitions. We were persuaded by audience feedback to remain faithful to our mission of staging plays with the choice of a dramatic metaphor that served to illuminate the dramatic action. "Wonder and delight" were built into every production. We made sure to introduce elements of "verve and sparkle" into every production, whether a tragedy by Shakespeare or a comedy by Bernard Shaw. My salary, by then, as an Assistant Professor in the Speech Department at the University of California, served to make up for the gap between even healthy ticket sales and our thrifty but elegant productions. Word about our always handsome productions got around so that even newspaper critics thought we were well subsidized by a wealthy Mother-in-Law from Kansas who fondly paid for every delightful whim of her gifted daughter, Suzanna, however extravagant and expensive it might be.

This absurd notion reached my ears right after we opened "Richard II" with its yards and yards of rich flowing Medieval and Renaissance costumes. Of course we never spoke up, ever, about how Suzanna had cornered the market in Goodwill Industries velvet velour draperies, saved for her all year by the manager of the Goodwill in nearby Oakland. Nor did we speak of Suzanna's perfected kitchen technique in first bleaching and then dying to her desired color, all the robes with their trains in "Richard II", for example. One carping critic who felt we were a bunch of "rich kids", spoke at a party with our Rhoda Nieman, playing the Duchess of York.. She asked Rhoda how much Suzanna "had to ask her mother for, to pay for the voluminous costume worn by Rhoda's Duchess?"

Rhoda told us the whole story. She said she replied, "My scene runs only about five minutes. So what makes you think Suzanna would spend a lot of money on my costume? I know for a fact that she spent a little over two dollars on it! She bought a pair of velour window draperies, all fully lined, from the Goodwill for two dollars, and then bleached out the rust color and dyed them that deep blue to make my gown with its train. But she first ripped out the worn sateen and used it as it was with its golden ecru color. Truth is I bitched when they showed me the original shabby draperies and said this was to be my beautiful gown. In the end I had to apologize, and we both laughed. When Mrs. Hart said, 'Well, in Kansa, I guess, Suzanna learned how to make a silk purse, ... or gown ... out of a sow's ear."

Thinking back to those seasons and productions leading up to 1957-58 there are some shows that are especially
memorable for the marriage of their dramatic action and
our dramatic metaphor. "The Knight of the Burning Pestle",
a hilarious Elizabethan comedy was designed with the King,
Queen, and Jack of modern day playing cards in mind. The
metaphor for "A Man for All Seasons" by Robert Bolt, was
the Holbein paintings of Henry VIII 's Court, come to life.
For Arthur Miller's "A View From the Bridge", we took our
cue from romantic, social realism of the '30's in the work
of painters like Charles Sheeler and Ben Shahn.

"Richard II" was, for us, one of the most challenging of
productions. We saw it as the final contest between the
Medieval culture, represented by Richard, himself, who
loses his throne and his life, and the newly emerging dynamic Renaissance represented by his aggressive cousin,
Bolingbroke, future Henry IV. The setting was a series of
platforms, small stages, really, built from the floor up, in-
creasing in height to four or five levels. As the play pro-
gresses, we see Richard in full royal regalia, on the upper-
most level, looking down on Bolingbroke and his men on
the lowest level of all. As the action unfolds, Richard is
gradually stripped, bit by bit, of his royal trappings, and is
seen in action each successive time, on lower and lower
levels. Bolingbroke on the other hand takes over as the
action unfolds, and each time he moves up from the stage
floor to reach Richard's earlier stages.

At the end, Richard is reduced to a simple purple gown,
wearing only the Order of the Golden Fleece (he is still,
but barely, the King), and sits on the lowest stage level,

where Shakespeare has him acknowledge his humanity with "For God's sake, let us sit upon the floor and tell sad tales of the death of kings..."

Soon after the holiday season, we opened "Murder in the Cathedral" by T.S. Eliot. I knew the play had been first produced in London in 1935 and enjoyed only a moderate success. I also recalled reading about the Federal Theater production in 1937. Suzanna and I had a serious talk about the budget for the play and the fact that it had never been a wild success, and might be a bit too intellectual for our audience. We agreed on a Spartan production and, I must confess now, that I selfishly insisted that our finances were such we could afford to indulge me. Suzanna, as usual, came up with some brilliant ideas about the set and costumes, and we knew we had some really strong actors. When I spoke to some of our actresses, they all said they'd love, for a change, to be part of a chorus. It would be an unusual and welcome experience. In fact, the play enjoyed a moderate success at the Playbox, better than we had anticipated, though nothing like our musicals and operas.

In mid-season, without any advance warning to us in our San Francisco theaters, nor to any of the theaters like ours in other American cities, Brooks Atkinson, distinguished critic of the **New York Times**, sent a letter to the theater critics on the major papers in about half a dozen cities from coast to coast to say the **Times** was sending him to report on the state of the American theater outside New York. Off-Broadway had made its mark by then, and Atkinson asked for recommendations as to what theaters he should see first hand way, way off Broadway.

In San Francisco, we five Resident Theaters, as we called ourselves, had formed a small organization to co-ordinate our programs more effectively and to collaborate in marketing our tickets. The chair revolved every year to each director in turn. In 1958, the chair came round to me, so I was the designated official host for Brooks Atkinson and his jolly, witty wife, Oriana. On their first evening in town, I picked them up at the Saint Francis Hotel on Union Square and suggested a schedule for the week so that each night he would see another of our theaters in action. I did what I thought was fair in scheduling so that the Golden Hind was neither first nor last. The fact is we didn't know in advance if he was going to write a single piece lumping us all together, or write an individual review for each theater and its production. It turned out he did write a separate review for each of us, and each review appeared on a separate day in the New York Times. He made it clear to us all, graciously and simply, that he was covering all our productions with the same professional eye he used when he reviewed shows on Broadway. We all readily and proudly accepted this compliment.

After the first production he saw, I picked up the Atkinsons for a drink, sensibly avoiding any questions or comments about what they had just seen; nor did Atkinson offer any. At the hotel bar we became fast friends. Indeed, it was the beginning of a friendship that lasted many years, first in San Francisco and later on in New York. We were a jolly group, and Suzanna and Oriana hit it off wonderfully well, laughing and joking, while Brooks and I, by now on a first name basis, talked about the season on Broadway, and various major theatrical issues.

For Atkinson's visit to the Golden Hind, I had chosen "Murder in the Cathedral" which was running then at the Playbox in Berkeley. Our Kenneth McClellan, who was so moving in his portrayal as Richard II the season before, was a most eloquent, spiritual, and courageous Thomas Becket. The chorus of women of Canterbury spoke the verse with clarity and passion, all the while communicating the fears and hopes of the ordinary folk they symbolized. They adapted quickly and easily to the choreographed movements I asked them to do, and they reached a group style and identity that served the play very well indeed, and held the audience's attention throughout. The reviews from the critics in town were decent, enthusiastic to a degree, but not enthralled; business was fair to good.

Two days after Brooks and Oriana saw "Murder in the Cathedral," I was in my office at the Bella Pacific when the telephone rang and I recognized the voice of Paine Knickerbocker, drama critic for the *San Francisco Chronicle*.

"Hi, Rachmael, this is Knick."

"Good morning, Knick," I answered.

"I have some good news I know will make you very happy."

"Thanks for calling with good news so early in the morning. What's the good news?"

"Here at the **Chronicle, we**'ve just had a story come over the wire from the **New York Times**. You ought to see it. I know you'll want to. Do you get the **Times?**"

"No, Knick, I don't," I replied. "Sometimes I pick up a copy on a Sunday when I'm being lazy all day in the house. I haven't seen today's paper."

"I think you should run, not walk, to the nearest news stand and get yourself a copy. Our distinguished visitor from New York..."

I interrupted, "You mean Brooks Atkinson?"

"Yes, I mean Brooks Atkinson. He's given you a terrific review for "Murder in the Cathedral." I have it here in front of me, so, congratulations."

"Thanks Knick. I'm running right out."

In a frenzy I rushed out to the nearest big newsstand where I knew I could pick up the paper, and frantically turned to the theater page. There on page twelve, with the heading, <u>The Theater: "Murder in the Cathedral" on Coast</u> was Brooks Atkinson's review of the production he had seen at the Playbox, with a handsome photo of Kenneth in costume. At the top of the first column was the heading, "Eliot Play Illumined by Berkeley Company." The review took note of everything about the production, acknowledging our actors, the set and costumes, the Playbox theater itself, and not leaving out the director and his staging.

The closing sentence of the review, which I quote here (throwing false modesty aside) follows:

> "Under the arched roof of an old laundry building, it (the play) retains poetic exaltation and spirituality and makes show business look shabbier than ever."

I called home where Suzanna was working in her studio on the next production and she came roaring down to join me. Knick printed the entire glowing review in the next day's **Chronicle,** and the box-office telephone started ringing madly with reservations that filled the house for the next few weeks. I sent out a call to every member of the company I could reach and we gathered together at the Playbox and toasted each other with Napa champagne.

The visit of Brooks Atkinson to San Francisco and points West seems to me to have marked a truly historic moment with national significance. It aroused in the public consciousness the importance of our emerging regional theaters. As our friendship blossomed, Brooks and I continued to exchange views about the new phenomenon of theaters springing up in cities across all America. He told me he thought of us all as "residential theater" (his words). He noted we were each taking our place in our own urban centers, but he didn't like the sound of "residential". He thought it might lead people to look on us as if we were a bunch of home bodies enjoying a hobby together. He decided to switch to "resident theater"; it carried a more professional stamp, he said. When I spoke up about what I saw as our heritage bequeathed by Hallie Flanagan and the Federal Theater, and her use of the term "grass roots theater." he sniffed at the phrase. He said it sounded like a bunch of hick framers putting on a show – not the right message. In the following year, when he came West to visit some cities he missed the previous years, he stopped to visit in San Francisco and did, in fact, refer to us as "grass roots" theaters.

We should keep in mind that Atkinson's visit occurred before public funding of the theater came into practice. There were a few exceptions where an enlightened town or city gave a small subsidy to local theater groups. Symphonies, opera companies and museums, and a few dance groups such as classical ballet companies were subsidized to a limited extent by public funds. Martha Graham, for instance had no public subsidies. She did have one true Angel who believed in her all through her long career. Her Angel was the Broadway stage star, Katharine Cornell with her producer husband, Guthrie McClintock. But the theater on the whole simply did not have the cultural cachet these other performing arts groups had. Theaters depended almost entirely on income from ticket sales, with limited funding from private sponsors to help cover the ever-present deficit. I'm sure there were many mothers-in-law across the country as big hearted as mine. Perhaps there were other influences at work at the time, but I've always thought it was Atkinson's tour of the regional theater scene that served as a major impetus to the original startling decision the Ford Foundation made later that season. For the first time since the Foundation undertook to subsidize the arts, it announced a new program funding theater companies such as ours, elevating our companies to the ranks of the other artistic ventures they deemed worthy of their support. It was Atkinson's national coverage of the work of the regional theaters which lit the fire that gradually transformed what were originally thought of as "little theaters" (code name for "amateur") into semi- and then fully professional theaters. These finally became the "grass roots" movement first envisioned 20 years earlier by President Roosevelt and his Federal Theater Director, Hallie Flanagan.

VI - The Bella Pacific

The sight of the Brooks Atkinson rave review of our "Murder in the Cathedral", reprinted in full in the **San Francisco Chronicle**, as soon as the review appeared in **The Times**, not only made my heart beat faster, it also whetted my appetite for a Golden Hind performing space in San Francisco. It is true our audience in Berkeley had grown through the years. 1957-58 was too early to enjoy the benefits of computers or e-mail access, so we created by hand our mailing list and subscription list, and by hand we typed each envelope, sent printed brochures by mail and, bit by bit, built our own audience. Each season saw an increase in ticket sales and in public attention. The open stage with our grand-piano shaped platform worked well, and we found we had a steady audience who readily accepted the intimacy of our 162 seats..

We exploited the open stage with success, and it found favor with the public, as the following account illustrates. I remember very well a late Saturday afternoon when I was sweeping the lobby and taking phone reservations for our first runaway success, a chamber production of Mozart's

"Cosi fan Tutte" sung in English. We had Berkeley's acclaimed Nathan Schwartz at the piano, and the role of Don Alfonso was sung by San Francisco's world class baritone, Edgar Jones.

A mild and gentle-looking grey-haired man came in the front door and smiled, "Good afternoon. I was hoping I'd find someone here so I can pick up our tickets for this evening before going to dinner. I suppose you must be Ben-Avram, the director here?"

"Yes, I am. How'd you guess?"

He answered with a friendly voice, "In my experience, when you see someone sweeping up while everyone else on the team is out to lunch, he's got to be the boss. The top man always cares more than anyone. At least that's the way it's been in my business."

"It's nice to hear that. Tell me your name please and I'll find your tickets so you can be off and enjoy your dinner. I'm sure you'll enjoy the performance. It's had wonderful audiences. Your name, please?"

"It's Nimitiz," he said, with no emphasis, and spelled it out, as if I needed it. "N I M I T Z."

"I know that name," I said. "I know how to spell it. Are you related, by any chance, to the Admiral?"

"Not by chance, young man. I am the Admiral."

"Admiral Nimitz, let me shake your hand. You're one of the true heroes of our time, if you'll allow me to say so. What an honor to have you in our theater tonight."

"Oh, we come here often, you know," he replied. "You see my wife has a hearing problem. In fact, so do I. And we really like coming here because your people always speak so clearly. We know we'll always be close enough to hear them. I guess you get them all to speak up?"

I answered, "Yes, I do. And you'll hear our singers tonight, clear as a bell. Especially when they know you're here."

As the Admiral picked up his tickets and handed me his check, he said, "Now don't go telling them I'm here and making them nervous. We live here in Berkeley you know, and we don't like to cause a fuss when we go out. But give them all my best. Thanks for the tickets. See you later."

Mozart was not hard to sell to the Berkeley audience. We soon found that our chamber productions of opera and musicals, every summer, were very strong at the box-office. We also noticed a surge in reservations from San Francisco when, at last, we were reviewed in the San Francisco daily press. However, our location in Berkeley worked against us as we reached out to the San Francisco public we hoped to attract in greater numbers. The critics from the two major dailies were obliged to cover almost any kind of performance in the City before putting us on their schedule. The theater critics, as well as the music critics, usually didn't come over the bridge to Berkeley until our second or third weekend. We couldn't help realize how much our box-office suffered. So the question in my mind was what we could do to improve our position on their schedule. The *Chronicle* and the *Examiner* were the two most important papers in San Francisco, reaching a large public in Berkeley as well as in the other San Francisco suburbs. The two most influential critics in the Bay Area wrote for these papers.

The problem of how to get timely coverage of our opening nights in these two leading newspapers became another of my store of obsessions. As the seasons went by, I had established friendly relations with Paine Knickerbocker of the **Chronicle**, and, when I asked him what we could do to expedite, facilitate, and encourage his attendance at our openings, he told me what I already knew.

"Frankly, Rachmael, it always seems such an extra chore to drive over the bridge to Berkeley, even if it's not all that far. Besides, we're a San Francisco paper, so almost any kind of performance in the City takes precedence with my editor. But I know you people are doing some excellent things, and I'll do what I can to come over sooner rather than later."

Our conversation served as a wake up call for me, and convinced me that I was right to decide that we had to have a theater in San Francisco itself. I was also aware, that for most people living in the Bay Area, driving into the City was not an obstacle to enjoying cultural pleasures such as the theater, the opera , the symphony, and dining out. Even driving over and back during the day for work, and then returning again for an evening event was not so daunting. But, for people living in San Francisco, driving over to Berkeley in the evening always seemed to them an unwelcome challenge: it loomed as large in their minds as a major water crossing and driving into the country. I could see no way to change their attitude on this score. I became convinced that the only way to resolve the problem of getting more media attention and developing a larger San Francisco audience was to find a second home in San Francisco for the Golden Hind.

And I did.

I found an old abandoned two story brick building situated right in the middle of what was once the famed, or rather the infamous, Barbary Coast. We all loved the idea of putting down roots in a part of the city with so enduring a disreputable reputation.

The idea of the Barbary Coast enchanted us all. Barbary Coast was the historic name for our Pacific Street. The building was still identified by its name when it had been operating as a cabaret, The Bella Pacific. Its address was 529 Pacific Street between Montgomery and Columbus Avenue, which is now the heart of the financial district, the Wall Street of San Francisco. At the time of the Gold Rush, the sailing ships bringing in the men and, in fewer numbers, women, to reap the rewards of the Gold Rush would dock in the bay at the foot of Pacific. In substantial numbers, the captain and crew often decided to join the Gold Rush and abandon ship. In time, these abandoned ships were buried beneath land fill and became part of what we now call North Beach. Almost from day to day, the shoreline was gradually pushed out from the end of lower Pacific Street and the neighboring streets until a sizeable district of five or six square blocks on either side of Pacific Street was marked out. Pacific Street was always the main drag, and bars and brothels abounded, welcoming the seamen and miners about to rush north and east from San Francisco to the inviting gold mines. One history book of the era informs us that in the Gold Rush days "Pacific Street was called Terrific Street."

In 1946 when I arrived as a student at U.C. Berkeley, Pacific Street was in the throes of being transformed and upgraded from being a haven of bars and honky tonk cabarets. The histories of the period celebrate some of the more notorious bars and night clubs, with The Black Cat getting its well-deserved share of attention. I recall my first New Year's Eve at Berkeley in 1946, when my poet friend Donald Thayer Bliss and I took the still functioning ferry (now long discontinued) from the Oakland Mole to the San Francisco Ferry Building at the foot of Market Street. We drank a bottle of cheap but good California red on the water, got a bit tipsy and sang to the seals in the Bay. Even today, it's a short walk from the Ferry Building to Pacific and Montgomery. There we pushed our way into the notorious, always swarming Black Cat Cafe, and joined in the singing around the jazz pianist at the upright piano on a small raised platform against the wall.

During World War II, most of the bars and brothels had been closed on Pacific Street, replaced by large Italian restaurants and cabarets with some of them providing a floor show. A decorative steel arch was erected over the intersections of Pacific at Columbus and at Montgomery, with blinking lights reading "International Settlement". Soon after World War II, a group of interior designers, and furniture and art importers got together and began to take over the original 19th century buildings in the area starting on nearby Jackson Street. To avoid the stigma of its sin-filled Gold Rush activities, these adventurous decorators and importers named the whole area, Jackson Square. It caught on and is still the center of fine and expensive furniture and art shops established by decorators, designers, and importers creating a very elegant community, a far cry from the old Barbary Coast.

One of the leaders of the new group was Bill Brewer, a good friend, specializing in Japanese imports; he thought we should have a Golden Hind playhouse in Jackson Square. A location on Pacific Street, he said, would be to our advantage; it would also reinforce the new image he and his colleagues were working to establish for Jackson Square.

Bill made some inquiries. Herman Miller, the furniture designer, had recently restored and renovated a brick building that had been a cabaret and night-club in the old days of the Barbary Coast. Its original name was The Bella Union, and his transformation created a unique showroom listed as a "must see" in all the tourist guidebooks. A few doors down from Herman Miller's Bella Union, Bill found us a vacant honky-tonk cabaret and we learned it had been called the Bella Pacific.

As soon as Bill told me about it, Suzanna and I drove over to see it with him and the owner. It was a brick building built around 1900, abandoned 15 years before. On its interior walls the sections of peeling plaster exposed the old rough brick inside and out. It was a style very popular in San Francisco during the 40's and 50's; today its exposed brick interiors have caught on in rehabilitated commercial areas in many American cities.

The interior had a large space on the street level where the floor show had been staged for the public who were seated at tables and chairs. We were quick to note there were functioning rest rooms to serve the public, though we saw they desperately needed gallons of disinfectant and deodorant and lots of decor. We saw we could adapt the space for the audience by installing ten rows of seats rising from the floor with steps at the end of each row to get the audience to their seats. We were able to create raised seating for an audience numbering 212 facing the stage from in front, as in most theaters. I preferred the Playbox with its open stage and seating on two sides, but we couldn't find a way to arrange that in the space we had. There was a good sized lobby as patrons came in the front door, with the acting area on the right. On the left of the lobby, there was a large square brick structure jutting out from the wall. We were told by the agreeable landlord that this structure was the support for an elevator, long gone, which was designed to get customers, some too tipsy to navigate, up stairs to the second floor. We climbed the stairs to the second floor to find a series of dingy little rooms, each with a window, a sink, and space enough for a small bed, night table and a chair. I couldn't imagine what use these small rooms could have had.

The landlord explained, "Oh, in the really old days, these were the cribs. That's what these rooms were. But that was long before my family took over."

"Cribs?" I said to Suzanna. "What kind of cribs would they be? What were babies doing up here?"

"Oh, honey," Suzanna said, poking me in the ribs. "Cribs for the whores. Don't you remember? That's what they're called?"

I did remember, and quickly dropped the subject. As a matter of fact, we had no use for the upstairs space and, of course, we needed to keep the rent down to a minimum so we passed on the upstairs space. Necessary, however, was the basement with its six dressing rooms with built-in dressing tables, and mirrors on the wall, framed in light bulbs. There were two toilets backstage for the cast, and stairs at the back of the building leading up to the main floor where we planned to perform. I remember so well that on that first visit we saw, written on a mirror with a red lipstick, "There'll never be another us." It was signed, Roxie. Suzanna and I agreed to keep the clean up crew from erasing Roxie's greeting until after the first opening night, just for luck.

We knew right away it was right for us, and Bill Brewer agreed heartily. We made it clear to the landlord we were NOT doing a strip show and we negotiated a manageable rent. The only work we had to do was to expose all the brick, give the interior a thorough cleaning, construct a box office, redo the rest rooms and create an appropriately charming decor. We also had to construct risers for 12 rows of theater seats, bring in the new/old theater seats from Pleasanton, as we did at the Playbox two years earlier, and hook up our new lighting console and spotlights. Around the brick elevator foundation, we set up a bar for beer and wine and soft drinks. Needless to say, we then spray-painted every wall and surface, sheetrock or brick, with Helen's Blue. Once again, Helen, as she had done for the Playbox, asked for the bill when I arrived from purchasing the paint and wrote us a check for the cost of the gallons and gallons of paint.

The landlord was decent and agreed to a lease which gave us two months rent free to complete our reconstruction and decor. The rectangular acting area faced the auditorium with no piano curve, so my staging was less interesting than at the Playbox. I regretted that. However,

I kept the stage open, with no curtain, and no separation between the acting area and the seating.

In most American cities it's not uncommon to hear it said, "You can't fight City Hall." San Francisco is no exception, But that's exactly what I had to do to open the Bella Pacific. The Playbox, meanwhile, continued with its schedule of eight productions for the year while simultaneously we faced the challenge of transforming a honky-tonk cabaret into a playhouse worthy of the plays and musical productions we produced. We were wildly optimistic about our future at the Bella Pacific, but there were days which made us fear that our grass roots would never grow and bring forth blossoms, especially since what seemed to be needed was ready cash, of which we had very little.

The Bella Pacific retained its name (but not, I hasten to add, its reputation), when I signed the lease soon after Atkinson's visit. At that time there were neither Federal nor State Councils on the Arts with subsidies for the theater, and no foundations to support the budding regional theater companies and their fledgling organizations. Consequently, we were all dependant on ticket sales to cover expenses, and family and friends for moral and occasional limited financial support.

I had anticipated the challenge of completely transforming the Bella Pacific, from the front of the house to the back wall, but was totally unprepared for the onslaught of the San Francisco Building Department and the Police Captain of our precinct.

Soon after we started work on the building, we had a visit from the City Building Inspector. Since we were not doing any work on the structure of the building, we had no need for a Building Permit. I explained to the Inspector that anyone could see we needed no building permit. We were merely adding some platforms and seats and creating a new décor. He asked to see the rest of the building. We were not leasing all of it, so we didn't have the key for the upper floor. However I did escort him downstairs to see the dressing rooms, and after some tense, silent moments he dropped his bombshell. According to the current building code, he told us, we couldn't possibly use the building for "public assembly" which was evidently our purpose, until the foundation had been reinforced to sustain an earthquake of a magnitude he mentioned. When I assured him that the building had withstood the earthquake of '06, not to mention several minor shocks since then, he shrugged his shoulders and said in essence, "the law is the law," and we were to let him know when the rehab work was completed.

Immediately I phoned one of our company members, George Conley, a successful businessman who loved to act small parts on our stage in his spare time. George understood right away what was up and put me in touch with a structural engineering firm on Montgomery Street. An engineer came down that day. I repeated the Inspector's demands and he explained to me that he understood the work the Inspector required and it would probably cost in the neighborhood of $20,000 and take a month to complete if I could find a contractor ready to start immediately. He added that he didn't think it was really necessary considering the age and solid condition of the building at present.

Hearing him put me into a sweat! I asked the engineer to speak to George and tell me what to do next. George called me the next day and said he'd come by and take me to one of his famous two Martini lunches, and suggest how we could proceed, short of $20,000. After the first Martini relieved some of the stress, George explained that the issue was political. I had to appreciate the reality that the Inspectors had a very stressful job, responsible for issuing Permits of Occupancy all over the city. It might be possible, George went on in a whisper, to assuage this man's stress if we could surreptitiously give him something to serve as a tranquilizer, say $200 or $300.

I understood completely, but where was I going to get my hands immediately on $200 in cash? I was sadly overdrawn at the bank in Berkeley, as usual. George, always the prince, said, "I'll see what I can do."

Two days later, the Inspector called to say he would like to review his previous inspection. Evidently, whatever George did was a success. When the Inspector arrived, we went down to the basement and he explained that he would take new measurements and he would review once more the anti-earthquake shock requirements. He mentioned that he had talked with our structural engineer, and would take some new measurements that might change things for us. He took out his tape measure, did some calculations and said he would send me a copy of his new report.

Two days later, the new report arrived, indicating that the building did, indeed, have enough "sheer" (was the word), and would withstand a shock within the limits of the law.

When I asked George if he had given the Inspector what he needed for his tranquility, he said, "Let's not bother with details. It's all set. However, you'll have to send a check for $200 as a fee for the engineering firm. They'll send a bill and you can pay it when you can."

In the midst of that perilous week, while we were still coping with the Building Department, the Precinct Police Captain dropped in for a chat. He spoke with a beguiling Irish brogue and a proper policeman's manner. He said he had seen our application for a beer and wine license and decided that he would block the application since, considering the location with its Barbary Coast history, he had concluded we would operating a Gay bar. Since the law prohibited Gay bars, he felt it was his job to withhold approval of our application for a license. To his mind, it was obvious we were going to become a Gay hangout. I explained that we were operating a serious theater, not a strip joint, and the bar was to serve only patrons of the theater. No one in San Francisco interested in a Gay bar would pay a $5.50 admission to the theater so he could buy a drink during the intermission and meet up with a prospective partner. He would certainly know a better place for a pick-up without spending $5.50 just to get in the door. The Captain was adamant, and with difficulty, I restrained my anger and frustration.

Was it Providence or our Karma that saved us in our conflict with the San Francisco Police Department? Three days after the Captain came to harass me, the **San Francisco Chronicle** printed a front page exposé of corruption at our precinct's Police Headquarters. The paper reported that it had been proven to the D.A. that most of the cops on duty in North Beach were shaking down the Gay bars in our area in exchange for ignoring them during their nightly surveillance. Most bars were handing out pay-offs once a week, some with even greater frequency, to keep open. Our Captain took early retirement the day after the exposé, and our beer and wine license was issued just in time for our opening.

I remember the panic at the opening night of the Bella Pacific. Curtain was at 8:30 and we were still painting the delightfully florid decor of the rest rooms a half hour before opening the theater doors. Richard Robinson and Jean Nowell, two of our gifted set designers, had decided on an elaborate decor, rather Erté-ish in style. The paint was on and fairly dry by 8:00 p.m. The programs arrived in time but, since they were wet with the printer's ink, we didn't distribute them until the intermission.

We opened the Bella Pacific with our long-running hit, the musical comedy that had been sold out at the Playbox in Berkeley for several months. It was "The Boy Friend," by Sandy Wilson, the show which had brought the unknown Julie Andrews to Broadway from London. Understandable pride spurs me on to say that our "The Boy Friend" ultimately ran for three years, in tandem with other productions on weekends, shifting back and forth between the Playbox and the Bella Pacific, as we needed.

Our plan was to open each new production in San Francisco, where, as I had hoped, we were generally reviewed the first weekend we opened. That production would run for six weeks in San Francisco before moving to the Playbox in Berkeley for another six weeks. Usually we had one dark week in order to make the shift from the Bella Pacific to the Playbox and to open the new production at the Bella Pacific, subject to occasional modifications in this schedule when it seemed necessary. Indeed, all said and done, our first season at the Bella Pacific, gave us the San Francisco identity we were looking for among the other resident companies in San Francisco.

VII - FORD'S BOUNTY

Our season of '57-'58 continued rolling on with yet another welcome surprise. Almost on the heels of the Atkinson visit and the opening of the Bella Pacific I received a letter which I took to be a very real confirmation of recognition in the big world for the grass roots theater movement to which I have referred so many times during this account. The letter was from the Ford Foundation, informing me that a gentleman by the name of Edward D'Armes, Associate Director of the Foundation's Program in Humanities and the Arts, would be coming to San Francisco to discuss the Foundation's interest in considering some form of support for the theater arts. The letter stated that this was a new interest at the Foundation, and would I please find some time to meet with him on his visit? Would I, indeed!

D'Armes soon arrived and we had a fairly long meeting, just the two of us. He asked me for suggestions as to how the Foundation could offer funding to support the development of theaters outside New York, theaters like ours and those of our growing number of grass roots colleagues across the country. The Foundation's concern was first, to be sure it would be contributing to the growth and evolution of the theater companies it subsidized. Secondly, the Foundation wanted to be sure that it would be explicitly understood that the grant would be a one time event, and by no means should any recipient theater embark on a project with the Foundation's money that could not be sustained on its own after the first year. That meant no capital improvements nor additions to the payroll that couldn't be carried through after the grant was spent.

I had a few suggestions which I candidly shared with Mr. d'Armes. I remember telling him that a very meaningful use of the grant might be to subsidize for one year the addition of a PR person to any theater staff, and presumably the PR staff person would generate sufficient additional income during that first year to sustain his or her salary the following year. I also suggested that part of the grant might be used to sustain a playwright in residence for one year. I went on with another suggestion, that they consider a grant to the founding directors of various companies outside New York, who were in situations similar to mine in San Francisco. Most theater companies had, indeed, been started up by some committed and passionately inspired person, usually a director who found he had a tiger by the tail once the theater got on its feet. I asked if the Ford Grant could be used for the director of such a theater to take a limited and busy sabbatical month or more to visit other countries, other cultures, even Broadway, to draw inspiration and stimulation from the experience of the other theaters, world-wide. I told him about the regional theater network in France, developed and subsidized by the government following World War II. I pointed out how rewarding it would be to attend the Festival of Ancient Greek Drama at Epidaurus, or the opera at Bayreuth where the grandsons of Wagner were creating modern and revolutionary productions of the Wagner operas, .following the precepts of theater art in the works by Gordon Craig and Adolphe Appia, even if that would turn Grandfather Richard in his grave. Referring to our post-naturalism work at the Golden Hind, I told d'Armes I wanted to study first hand the authentic traditional Japanese theater.

Our conversation came to a close with Mr. d'Armes making final notes on his yellow pad before thanking me for my time and input. It was almost summer and we were up to our ears planning our next season. Perhaps a month passed after D'Armes's visit, when I had another letter from the Ford Foundation. This was from Mr. McNeil Lowry, Director for the Program in Humanities and the Arts. He announced that the Foundation had decided to make 10 grants of $10,000 each, to ten directors of resident theater companies outside New York. These would be the first-ever grants to be made to the theater. The grants would be awarded based on nominations of viable candidates by a search committee of approximately 300 persons active in the theater across the country, persons such as myself. I was asked to please send in my anonymous nomination of one or more individuals I felt were deserving of such a grant, who would were sure to make good use of it. No direct applications would be accepted. Candidates to be considered would be selected only from the nominations received from the aforementioned committee. The nominators were to remain anonymous. I was advised to respond within the fortnight, and was given instructions how to do so.

I must confess the letter put me into a terrible state. I was, of course, understandably proud and honored to see the Ford Foundation seriously consider my suggestions along with those others they accepted from other sources. I was honored to be included in the nominating committee. Of course, I wondered how many other theater contacts in the Bay Area had received a similar letter, and who would be the lucky ones to be nominated. I must confess that the green-eyed monster, Envy, caught me in her grip as I repeated over and over again, through gritted teeth, "No direct applications will be accepted."

How I wanted that grant! I asked around to find out who else had received the letter asking for nominations. Maybe I could weasel my way onto some other person's list of candidates. I asked around, discretely of course, and so far as I could learn, no-one I knew in the Bay area had even heard about these requests from the Ford Foundation. Of course I had to be very careful to guard my own anonymity as an honest nominator. My friend at the **Chronicle**, Knickerbocker, knew nothing about the grants. Almost at once he ferreted out my admission that I was, indeed, one of the distinguished 300. He laughed at my squirming and assured me I must be far better known in New York than he, to be on the nationwide search committee.

In the end, with difficulty, I mastered my envy as best I could. I accepted my responsibility to the cause of theater art. The truth is, I can now reveal, I nominated some one I fairly loathed, one of our chief competitors in San Francisco. As of now, more than 50 years have passed, so I think I can now admit I nominated Herbert Blau, one of the co-directors of the Actors' Workshop, a theater company that was diametrically opposed to the anti-realism we at the Golden Hind believed in. In matters of style and sincerity, they were always sincere, -- and to my mind boring. But no matter. There were two co-directors at the Actors' Workshop, and I knew them both to be hard working, committed to their vision for their own theater, even if they were as anti-Golden Hind as I was anti-Actors Workshop. I sent in Herb's name, and kept my nose to my own private grindstone.

Two months passed and again another unexpected letter from the Ford Foundation arrived to inform me that I was one of the eligible nominees!!!! Who in the world, I wondered, could have known my work and chosen to nominate me. I wondered without success. I could not think of a soul. (Only many years later, when I had moved to New York, I guessed it must have been Brooks Atkinson, when I heard he was on the Select Committee at the Foundation. I would never mention my surmise to him, but I did whisper my hunch to his wife, Oriana, and she said nothing but winked and bobbed her head up and down).

I lost no time in replying. I wrote that if I were to receive the grant I would plan to spend a week each, visiting our original sources of inspiration at the *Comédie de*

St. Etienne in France; the opera at Glyndebourne in England; Bayreuth in Germany; the classical theater in Greece; and the traditional theater in Japan. Ten days later my proposal was accepted and the grant arrived.

News of the Ford Foundation Grant for Theater Directors was covered by the New York Times, which listed the ten directors from all over the country, and I was feeling as much honored by the association with the others as I was by the grant itself. It took some doing for me to arrange for our two playhouses to keep functioning in my absence, but I recognized, perhaps even rationalized, that the necessities of making those arrangements had its positive side. It forced me to recast my view of our company management structure. I had to create a new organization plan so that I could, with good conscience, leave for a whole month, without having the company come to a standstill. Joan, our very able and very responsible Office Manager took over all the various responsibilities that were mine. I promised to phone in every other day from wherever we were, and when I did so, she gave me all the assurance I could want to enjoy the trip and benefits I expected from it.

The month's sabbatical was stretched to six weeks, and was as rewarding as we hoped. At every stop we found inspiration to continue our work, and encouragement to pursue our dream. The whole trip was a source of affirmation of our commitment to create what, to borrow a phrase from Thornton Wilder, was a "mythic theater experience." Wherever we visited, we saw each country's premier national theater, where the visual effects on stage and the intense focus of the staging and acting, reminded us that the influence of our mentors, as I have written of them above, was as evident in the work of the current contemporary theater in Europe, as it was in our work at our modest Playbox and Bella Pacific.

Our first stop was London where we saw the Old Vic with its stellar resident company of British trained actors. They served to reinforce my feelings that we must have a resident acting company creating a single ensemble performance for every production.

Our next destination was Athens. We flew there and found a hotel not far from the Acropolis and the Parthenon. This was in 1959, and we could easily walk around all the ancient temple ruins, touching them, sitting on them and avoiding marring them, as so many unthinking tourists had been doing to these ancient ruins for centuries. Our principal destination in Greece was Nauplia, in the Peloponnesus, a few miles from the ancient theater at Epidaurus. As we had planned, we were there during the Festival of Ancient Greek Drama. We found a small hotel overlooking the picturesque harbor and arranged to visit the very impressive remains of the theater at Epidaurus our first day. We came back to our hotel for dinner, returning to the theater in the evening to see the performance.

We were told by our hotel host that the best way to be sure of getting to the theater in time was to jump onto an open truck coming down the road toward us and join all the young town folk driving out there. We arrived in good time, enjoyed talking with some students on the truck who spoke English, and were soon in our bleacher seats for the first play, Sophocles's "Antigone". It was to be followed by "Oedipus at Colonnus" and then the comedy by Aristophanes, "The Frogs".

We saw the theater filled with about four hundred soldiers in military dress, some officers, by their uniforms, plus thousands of people, ordinary people from the farms and countryside villages. We wondered if a festival of ancient theater in our country would attract a similar audience. (Of course similar events now take place all over the United States; the Shakespeare Festivals we find in almost every state in the union). We were sitting next to some college students who spoke English and they explained that this was the most important Greek theater in the country. The Festival was subsidized by the government, and since the plays were performed in the original ancient Greek no longer spoken, no one in the audience could understand the dialog any better than we Americans. "Antigone" and "Oedipus at Colonnus" were familiar to us from our university studies of Greek theater, and the performances were very moving, even in the ancient Greek.

Aristophanes' "The Frogs" was a surprise. We didn't know it as well as the tragedies, and found it deliciously, blatantly bawdy, staged and acted with such energy and rowdy imagination it had the whole theater shaking with laughter at the mad antics between Euripides and Sophocles as they quarreled about who deserved most to be chosen by the Gods as the greatest of Greek playwrights, the theme of the play.

Glyndebourne, England, was our next stop, unforgettable and unique. I had arranged back home to buy a Triumph

TR3 convertible, an English sports car, in England, so we could drive around Europe. Sure enough it was ready for us in London. We planned to drive all over Europe and then ship the car home from London at the end of our tour. With the dollar very strong in those days, this plan was the most enjoyable possible and, the most economic.

Glyndebourne was noted for its intimate opera productions, especially the Mozart, and we knew the whole story about the jewel of an opera house of about 600 seats which a rich and loving husband built on his country estate for his wife, a gifted English soprano. It had opened in 1939. Situated in the country about 1½ hours from London by train, the Glyndebourne Opera still continues its summer opera festival with a first rate orchestra that comes down from London for the season. With such a small house, the tickets have always been quite expensive, but we were told, even school teachers, with their meager pay, save all year to be able to attend one or two of the four productions included every season. From that its very first performance in 1939, the Glyndebourne Opera has enjoyed a reputation as a world class opera company.

The opera had a restaurant on the premises, a converted old barn, called Nether Wallop Hall, and each production included a long 1½ hour intermission so the fashionable audience could dine comfortably. That accounted for the curtain going up at 4:00 p.m., almost the middle of the afternoon. As for dinner at the "interval," as the English call the intermission, we had a choice of reserving a table months in advance, as we did, when ordering tickets from San Francisco, or you could choose to enjoy a picnic of

your own, al fresco, in the cool summer air. When our opera tickets arrived in the mail, we found a note informing
us that the audience generally "dressed in dinner clothes",
and we took heed and packed at least one appropriate
outfit for each of us.

I have a vivid memory of Suzanna and me, in our little
sports car with the top down. She in her very becoming
green silk cocktail dress, and I in my tuxedo and black tie,
driving through the farmland, with all those farm animals
staring quizzically at us. Parking was arranged in the Sheep's
Meadow. This was aptly named since a very insubstantial
barrier separated us from about 30 head of sheep staring
across the hedges. looking completely bored. We noticed,
as we parked, a rather large number of Rolls Royces which
had already taken the best parking spaces. Some were em-
blazoned with a coronet or coat of arms on the hood.
Most of them had the rear trunk opened, with a built in
folding table dressed in white linen. At most of them we
could see a butler standing by with a champagne bottle in
hand, pouring for the elegant and smart looking group of
people nearby.

We had seats for "The Marriage of Figaro" and "Fidelio".
Through the Ford Foundation, I had a letter of introduc-
tion to the Director of the opera, Peter Ebert, son of Carl
Ebert who came to Glyndebourne soon after he had fled
the Nazi regime in Germany and had preceded his son as
General Director for some years.

The performances were beautifully sung and the staging lively, with young and talented singers from all over
Europe who spent the entire summer together, rehearsing

and performing. The productions were beautifully designed, though not quite as liberated from the old- fashioned opera stage decor as we liked. But, indeed, we were struck by the vitality and ensemble of the singing and acting.

During the long intermission in the middle of "Figaro", after a dreary, tasteless dinner at Nether Wallop Hall, we came back to our seats, well placed in the tenth row center. As we were early for the third act, we kept standing as the audience slowly began to file in. We had noticed all the women in their elegant finery, and remarked discretely to each other that some of the elegance had signs of having been in mothballs since before the war. However, at one moment my eye caught a very richly bejeweled, elegant looking woman of a certain age, in a stunning evening gown, designed, we thought, to make her look like a queen. In addition to the modest diamonds around her neck and at her ears, she wore a small diamond coronet which looked as if it were made for her. She walked up the aisle holding her short train, with a gentleman at her side, past us, smiling, not making any eye contact but moving forward slowly and steadily. When she got to the last row in the orchestra, she turned and connected with the audience, by now standing and looking after her. Then she raised her hand and gave us what everyone must have recognized, as I did, a royal salutation. We all put our hands together as if to applaud, but curiously, we seemed to agree spontaneously not to make a sound. It was, indeed, Her Majesty, the Queen Mother Elizabeth, who then turned toward the back of the house and walked up through the doors leading to the royal box.

As we were sitting down, the gentleman on my right turned and said, "Of course you know that was the Queen Mother, and you see how gracious she was to make that promenade for our sake so that tomorrow when we read in the papers she had been at Glyndebourne tonight, we could say to our grandchildren that we had seen her."

I started to turn my head, and he put his hand on my arm, "And of course you understand we respect her privacy, and none of us will turn to stare at her. We wouldn't wish to intrude on her pleasures here at the opera."

I felt stupid, but he saved me from making a social blunder.

Our next adventure was to cross the Channel on the ferry and drive down from Calais to Paris. Paris was as thrilling for us as when we first found each other there in 1949. Our first night out was at the *Comédie Française*, admiring the impressive elegance and grand style the French actors brought to everything they acted. It reinforced my obsession that all our actors learn to walk, to sit and stand, and wear period costumes, wigs, and gloves, as if they were born wearing them, and that they speak up and out reaching to the last row.

That summer in Paris we also saw what were probably Josephine Baker's last performances. She was doing a farewell production of a musical based on her life, "*Paris, Mes Amours*" (Paris, My Loves). In the first scene we saw Baker getting her start in St. Louis vaudeville. In the second scene we see her arriving in Paris. It was the largest part of the show taking place in Paris, that grabbed us. So French, so exuberant, so much feather boa in every number. We knew she was in her sixties, but her vitality was infectious. Talk about verve and sparkle! She wore flesh tights, her legs as shapely as if she were still in her twenties. She did her old routines, including the most famous of them all, with bananas hanging from her waist, on a runway that extended out into the audience just as they do, or did, in the strip shows in the burlesque theaters. And she wore feathers adorning every possible part of her anatomy. Nor did she stint on having the entire cast in feather boas from one scene to the next. She brought the house down every night for the whole month she was at the Olympia.

After Paris we went to Bayreuth and then for a few days to Munich. The opera house built for Wagner at Bayreuth was still functioning, a remarkable building. Built almost entirely of wood, the seating curves around the auditorium with access only from the sides, with no center aisles. Thanks to the wood used everywhere, the entire hall was itself a resonating musical instrument and we were engulfed by the sound.

We found a small hotel near the opera house and after checking in, I left Suzanna to wander around near the hotel. Tickets in hand, crossing the parking lot at the opera house, I bumped into Henry Boettcher, who had headed the Theater Department at Carnegie Tech when I was there. We fell into each others arms. I explained how and why Suzanna and I were there. He explained that he had recently retired and was coming back to Germany for the first time since his student days before World War II. He was quite alone and invited us to join him for the intermissions and meals that evening.

The Wagner brothers, Wolfgang and Wieland, Richard Wagner's grandsons , created settings which in some way we could call "minimal". They did not try to fill the stage with scenery. For each production they chose a single architectural element, discarding all else from the scene. In "Meistersinger" for instance, the great cathedral in Nurenburg was represented by an enormous, richly decorated, gold encrusted piece of the cathedral choir. In the second act, the medieval market place was overwhelmed by sitting under the top of a mighty flourishing oak tree, cut off , hanging in space above the tilted disc, serving as a canopy over a few simple market place stalls., Hans Sachs was hammering away at his shoes outdoors under the tree. Each element of the decor beautifully designed and richly decorated, giving the whole stage a mystical reality. In fact, what we saw was impeccable execution of what we could only modestly dream of suggesting at the Golden Hind. Everything at Bayreuth was rich and magnificent. We saw the ultimate manifestation of the inspiration of Gordon Craig and Adolphe Appia. To my mind, their work exemplified beautifully what Thornton Wilder referred to as a "mythical ambience", and was exactly suited to Wagner's text and music. The costumes were rich but simple in design, and gorgeously and imaginatively accentuated with accessories. The singers came on stage, monumental figures, sculptures come to life. We were almost breathless with excitement when we saw the lights go up. Here were stage productions that were essentially architectural rather than painted flats. This was no imitation of nature, but rather an evocation of a mythical environment in which heroic figures lived and breathed.

By the time we came home, we were ready to draw on our travel experiences. That first season after the European journey included "King Lear" with the metaphor of 12th century Cornwall church sculpture come to life on the "tilted disc" which the Wagner's had introduced in their productions. The tilted disc was a kind of stage on the stage, and provided a special, almost magical, point of focus for various scenes where it served the production well. For Lear we had the actor who had played Thomas Becket in "Murder in the Cathedral," our Kenneth McClellan , and he soared in the role, and I wished that Brooks might have seen him in Lear after his reaction to Kenneth's Becket.

For a musical that summer, I chose Harold Arlen's "House of Flowers" which we knew from its commercial recording by the original Broadway cast. I read the press reviews in which all seemed to agree that the show had been overproduced on Broadway. We agreed with the critics that this was probably Arlen's best score ever. The musical with words by Truman Capote was based on a short story by Capote about a house of prostitution on a small mythical Caribbean island. We were able to find a multi-ethnic cast of singers and dancers in the Bay Area who came out of nowhere to join us when they heard we were staging "House of Flowers". Suzanna and I agreed that the principal role could have been created for a young Josephine Baker, and the whole production looked as if the cast had come down from a seductive travel poster for a Caribbean vacation. She dressed the cast in Caribbean colors, and I remember paying for hundreds of yards of feather boa, in which the dancers flounced around and absolutely captivated the audience.

The first night remains especially memorable. We opened at the Bella Pacific with a small three piece combo on stage doing the music. Some of our cast who had appeared in "The Boy Friend" were in the show, together with our Afro-American and Hispanic singers and dancers. Stanley Eichelbaum, the drama critic for the **San Francisco Examiner**, Knickerbocker's colleague in arms on the competing paper, came to the first night as usual. He phoned me in advance to tell me he was bringing Arnold Saint-Subber, the Broadway producer of the original "House of Flowers" which had lasted no more than two months on Broadway and lost a fortune for its investors. At the intermission, I went out to welcome Saint-Subber and found that he and Stanley were both almost delirious about the production. Just before we went into the second act, he turned to Stanley and me and said,

"Stanley, you see Mr. ben-Avram has really worked his magic here. In New York we had all the money we wanted, we had Peter Brooks directing, we had Oliver Messel for set and costumes, Herbert Ross did the dances and musical numbers, and the cast had Diahann Carroll as the main character with Pearl Bailey as Madame Fleur. Everybody we had was a somebody on Broadway. All together we thought we knew what a musical should be and we thought we would really please everybody. Mr. ben-Avram here, and his cohorts, only set out to please themselves, and that's what they did. The result is that while we pleased nobody, these people here are pleasing everybody."

At the end of the show I went out to say goodbye to Saint-Subber, and he startled me by asking if I would consider coming to New York and staging an off-Broadway production of "House of Flowers" for him. It was a proposal that put me into a turmoil. I asked if I could think about it for a day or two. I talked to Suzanna about it, but it hardly took any time to realize what my answer had to be. I was well aware that the earlier trip to Europe put a strain on the company that almost put it out of existence. I knew in my heart that I just couldn't go to New York for the months needed to create another "House of Flowers". I would be abandoning my own theater company, my own family, my own vision that had kept me going and had really been the source of my energy and my bliss.

The next day I told Saint-Subber that I appreciated his invitation, but I couldn't see any way to leave my theater for the time it would take to do the show in New York. With much regret I had to tell him no.

"House of Flowers" was another great hit for the Golden Hind. After the opening I was able to allow myself to recognize my flagging energies and a need for a more vigorous flow in creative juices. In hindsight, of course, I was in the throes of burn-out.

I recognized that my own personal verve was losing its sparkle, and it was time for an infusion of new energy. There were other issues surfacing in our life, Suzanna's and mine. For ten years we had spent almost 24 hours a day in each other's company, at work and at play, at home and at the theater. The stress we experienced in the normal course of creating our Golden Hind productions was usually resolved by the next opening night. Truthfully, we had enormous respect for each other's judgments and opinions, and, as I remember it, we always found our way to a harmonious resolution of any differences. At home, we were a family, and often swept our disagreements or expectations of each other under the rug. After ten years together, that rug got to be a little lumpy and signs of wear began to show. We looked for professional counseling of course , after all we were living in San Francisco, and eventually accepted the reality that while we were still together in all ways at the theater, at home we were more and more disengaged. We had, in fact, been growing apart. Because we still felt mutual respect and admiration, and indeed, affection, we agreed we both wanted a separation while we were still talking to each other as caring friends, before we started throwing dishes and pots and pans across the kitchen floor. Indeed, we remain to this day (some 50 years later) as caring about each other as ever.

There was still the trip to Japan in store as part of the Ford Foundation Grant. When I said I wanted to go to Japan on my own, Suzanna told me quite frankly she was relieved to hear it. She didn't want to make the trip at all. We went much further in talking about our feelings and came to an agreement that she would move out of our house, as she wanted, by the time I returned from Japan. With this clearing of the air, we planned to go on working together as before. My heart, however, was heavy.

I arrived in Tokyo with a letter of introduction to the chairman of the Japanese Office of the International Theater Institute. Without knowing a word of Japanese, nor a single soul in Tokyo, I was able to have the doorman at my hotel put me in a taxi and send me off to the Kabuki-za, the main Kabuki theater. By a set of very happy circumstances, and after many instances of miscommunications with people at the hotel and at the theater, I chanced to meet up with a young man who worked for a big pharmaceutical house in Tokyo as their English business correspondent. Hirotake-san was surprised that I had come all the way to Tokyo from San Francisco to observe and study the classical Japanese theater without even knowing a word of Japanese. He spoke English fairly well, and informed me almost immediately we met, that he was a passionate and knowledgeable fan of the traditional Kabuki theater. He was delighted to offer his assistance as my personal guide to the Kabuki, and at the same time, improve his spoken English by spending so much time with me. With his help, I finally met the Secretary of the International Theatre Institute for Japan, Nabeshima-san, who spoke some sparse English, but French fluently, and we got on in French. He offered to introduce me to the various Japanese theater traditions and forms, -- Kabuki, Noh, and Bunraku Puppet Theater, including some visits backstage. For my weeks in Japan, I split my time and attention between these two heaven-sent guides.

I had prepared for this trip by reading up on the three major traditions, the Kabuki, Noh, and Bunraku, but learning the language was beyond hope. However, though I understood not a word, the acting at each performance was of such a high, intense level that I found I could follow the plays and understand the action even without the language. It was fatiguing but I went to the theater with one or the other of my new comrades at least once every day, sometimes twice,-- matinee and evening. The matinees in Tokyo always started around noon, with several intermissions for lunch and tea, ending around 4:30 p.m. A completely different program for the evening performance started at 6:00 p.m. and ended by 11:00. The same Kabuki actors did two completely different shows in one day, acting almost ten hours a day all together. Perhaps this accounted in part for their impressive acting skills which, to me, served to confirm what I knew of Stanislavsky's method and Stasberg's Actors' Studio teaching. Even without the language, the Japanese acting skills communicated the authenticity of the characterizations and the complete commitment on the part of the actors to revealing the inner life of the role they were playing on stage. I surmised that the Japanese theater had been honing these skills for centuries, long before the Moscow Art and the Actor's Studio were even thought of.

The programs never gave us a complete ten or twelve act play in its original ancient form. Contemporary programs always were composed of "highlights" from some of the great Kabuki classics. To relate this to our Western theater practice, imagine a performance on an American stage, starting off with the Balcony Scene from "Romeo and Juliet" followed by the Graveyard Scene from "Hamlet", then the last act of "King Lear", and so on. The Kabuki audiences were familiar with the scenes on the program and were very keen to compare and appreciate the nuances and accomplishments of the actors just as we would enjoy weighing a Gielgud Hamlet against an Olivier Hamlet.

After attending a few performances by the Grand Kabuki and several other smaller, touring companies, I asked my theater guide, Nabeshima-san to explain what element in the movements, the vocalizations, the make-up and costumes, what exactly did the audience see in the performance that evoked their occasional shouts and loud exclamations of approval. I learned that the Japanese public never applaud in the theater. Actually, it is the actors who applaud the audience. They all come forward on the stage after the final performance of the usual 28-31 days of a run and acknowledge the audience by applauding us, as a way of saying thank you.

To my question, Nabeshima said, "But Rachmael-san, all that you admire about the movement, the costumes, and the staging, is superficial. Actors spend their whole life acting the great roles, and they learn as apprentices all the very stylized moves and rhythms of the staging. What they also learn from the senior actors to whom they are apprenticed is the art of acting, exposing the character's inner life. What we in the audience look for when we look for excellence, for truly great acting, we look to find in the actors' eyes. There we see the depth of his characterization and his artistic sensibilities. Don't you have a saying in English, -- 'The eyes are the mirror of the soul'?"

His simple statement opened my eyes, and I realized that this was the reason I could understand all the acting and interaction between the actors in the Japanese theater. It gave me much to think about and bring home to our Golden Hind.

Nabeshima-san introduced me to the much more restrained, almost suppressed Noh theater, performed with masks, and to the Bunraku Puppet Theater. We went backstage on several occasions and the actors responded to my questions about their stage traditions very generously.

My sojourn to Japan was limited mostly to Tokyo, Kyoto, and Osaka for the classical forms of theater. I did see one performance of a play about Hiroshima. The young actors performed with great intensity, and reminded me of Strasberg's comment about "getting on the streetcar". I also included Takarazaka, a special kind of resort where the central attraction was a huge theater where you could experience the elaborate all-girl musicals with a cast of hundreds. It was so extravagant, so loud, so romantic. And it all came from the Japanese desire to emulate the big Broadway musical.

In Kyoto, rather than attending a Kabuki or Noh performance, I went to hear the professional story-tellers, carrying on a tradition dating from medieval times. It was almost like hearing a recitation of "The Canterbury Tales". In Osaka I saw the National Bunraku Theater, the puppet theater with a three hundred year tradition. It was my good fortune to be present at a performance by the great blind Master Puppeteer who was still alive that year, performing at his theater with superb skill and vitality even though he was then in his eightieth year and completely blind. I learned that he had been honored by the Emperor and designated a National Treasure, as if he were some great work of art, which I guess, in truth, he was.

It came as something of a surprise to me to realize that what I learned about acting from the Japanese theater served to reinforce the lessons learned at the Actors' Studio with Lee Strasberg, and from the writings of Stanislavsky and Gordon Craig.

I recognized that what we had developed as our Golden Hind style in acting had some kinship with the living theater of Japan. In the plane coming home to San Francisco, I gave thanks to the Ford Foundation for fulfilling my expectations as much as I could have wished.

VIII - WITH MUSIC
AT THE CLOSE

When I returned home to San Francisco, I found we were losing ground in both theaters. Box-office receipts were really falling. Suzanna had moved out of our house and into her own apartment and her new life on her own, but we both knew how much we depended on each other for the creative part of our lives, and it was time to get to work.

It wasn't planned that way but our tenth season turned out to be our last season. I had heard the recording of Bernstein's "Candide" which opened on Broadway with Barbara Cook as Cunegonde. Listed as a musical comedy, but perhaps closer in form to an opera, it closed after a short run on Broadway. I loved the recording by the original cast and decided we could do a staged concert production, if I could get the rights.

It was impossible to get anyone in New York representing the rights to the performances to respond to my calls, so I flew to New York and was informed by the agency controlling royalties that I could get a piano score and a script from them but I would have to get the rights to a performance from Leonard Bernstein himself. I suppose there was an Angel on my shoulder because among my acquaintance someone had the telephone number for Bernstein's apartment in New York, and I got through by phone. I think it was his wife who answered, and she responded to my earnest and eager request for a brief interview with him about "Candide" by advising me that he was rehearsing the symphony that afternoon at Carnegie Hall and the best shot I had of talking to him was to catch him at the break. I thanked her heartily, ran quickly to Carnegie Hall and managed to get though the doors to the auditorium while the orchestra was rehearsing. I sat in a back row, trying to look like someone quite accustomed to sitting in the back row waiting for the Maestro to stop for a break.

After sitting still with a pounding heart for almost a half hour, I heard a voice say "Take a break". Bernstein came down off his podium and stood talking on stage with some individuals who needed his attention. I briskly walked down to the stage and jumped up onto it so that he could see I was there, waiting to see him. He finished his conversation with whomever and looked at me, so I joined him. I introduced myself, told him I wanted the rights to do "Candide" in San Francisco in a concert version and that I needed his approval, if he would be so kind. If he was startled by my chutzpah, a quality he knew very well in himself, he didn't show it. He quickly told me he approved, but that I needed Lillian Hellman, who wrote the book, and Richard Wilbur, the poet who wrote most of the lyrics, to agree as well.

I asked him how to get that. And he gave me the name and address of his attorney who was in charge of such matters and told me to send the attorney a letter of request, and he, Leonard Bernstein, would talk to him and ask him to get the other approvals needed. I thanked him mightily, seeing a few others in a line behind me waiting to talk him. I left with high hopes and a very light heart. I'm happy to say, it all turned out as he promised.

When I began to put together a production of "Candid," I fortuitously met Lou Huber, a well rounded musician, teaching at San Francisco State College. Lou agreed to make an arrangement for piano and combo of three other musicians and take on the work of Music Director. We held open auditions, and we actually found a soprano who could hit the high E as needed in the Jewel Song.

For Suzanna and me this would be our last production together, though neither of us even tried to acknowledge it until we were through the opening night. "Candide" was certainly one of our greatest successes. A faithful theatergoer, Mr. Philip Lilienthal, was there with his wife on opening night and was so taken with our simple production he came looking for me at our Post-Performance Champagne Celebration.

"Rachmael" he said, "you know I was one of the backers of the Broadway production that Tyrone Guthrie directed, and we lost our shirt. I must have lost over $30,000. on it. I'll bet you didn't have to spend half that much for the whole show here at the Bella Pacific, did you?"

"Mr. Lilienthal," I replied, "to tell you the truth, our whole budget for the show was just a bit over $3,500."

"Well, Rachmael," he went on, "I guess I should have bank-rolled you.

I would have gotten more for my money, knowing I had helped make it happen."

The Golden Hind production was offered as a concert version with six women and six men in the chorus, plus the principals. It was simple but not static. The men wore black tie and tuxedo, while the women were dressed in an evening gown designed by Suzanna, with each singer wearing a different color of the same gown. She also designed some costume accessories and some hand props to suggest the change of place and time as the show progressed.

We did not create a changing set, nor did we change costumes for each change in scene. I did not seat the principals and chorus on a bare stage and just let them stand and sing the witty lyrics and beautiful music. Suzanna and I applied our usual working methods, even to this concert staging. We came up with one of our simplest, and yet, most effective metaphors for the production. There in the middle of our stage we constructed a giant wooden wedding cake, large and solid enough to support the weight of the singing actors as they performed the story by Voltaire about Candide's journey through life and his final reunion with his true love, Cunegonde. In pursuing his fortunes life. In pursuing his fortunes through various perilous adventures, he never loses faith and continues to face each disaster with the philosophic view his teacher, the philosopher, Dr, Pangloss, taught him. He keeps singing --- "This is the best of all possible worlds".

In our production, the show opened with Candide and his bride Cunegonde atop the wedding cake looking like a living wedding cake decoration, holding branches of apple blossoms arched over their heads. The chorus occupied the lower layers of the giant cake and sang their praises of the married couple. As the show goes on, the lovers are separated by war and misfortune and we see them wander through their ups and downs, always connected to the wedding cake with its scenic accessories suggesting the different cities in the world to which fortune brings them. The dialog and musical numbers, enhanced by means of the imaginative use of symbolic props and costume accessories, made it possible to follow the narrative without difficulty. Winding their way around the giant wedding cake, and never totally destroyed by the dangers encountered, the lovers are finally reunited and join hands agreeing to "build our house and chop our wood and make our garden grow" -- the words in Bernstein's powerfully moving final chorale with which the piece ends.

After ten years of working together, Suzanna and I usually had little more about the production to discuss by the time we got to the dress rehearsals, except perhaps to review some minor concerns about costumes, lighting, and other details. For opening nights, she usually arrived in time for the final act so she could then join the cast after the final curtain, sip champagne and refreshments and shower the cast and crew with congratulations. For "Candide", however, she was on hand all through the last several run-throughs, and told me how much she liked what we had achieved together. On opening night, I saw her enter the theater and take an empty seat in the last row, near the aisle. I was very pleased to see her sit once again through the whole show, and, at the same time, very sad.

At the last curtain call, Suzanna came over to me and told me the staging was "brilliant", an unusual comment since we almost never traded compliments in so many words. She remarked that it was obviously a wonderful experience for the audience who "ate it up." Then she said, sadly, she said she didn't think she had any more energy to do the next show. She went on to say that, of course, she knew I would understand and find a way to survive. I always did, didn't I? I nodded.

I stayed until it was time to lock up the theater and drove off to a favorite bar to sip a cognac or two in quiet, and reflect on the current affairs in my life and in the life of the Company of the Golden Hind.

The rift with Suzanna brought to mind the Bernstein choral ending to "Candide" and the telling words he set to his stirring music. I could easily believe, as we later learned in his biography, that he had written these words — as well as the music — when his own domestic peace was in turmoil. I felt abandoned and lost. An inner voice told me that I had to do more than offer this winning production of "Candide" to Suzanna as a Valentine if I wanted to persuade her that we might succeed in building a brighter future out of what we'd learned from our hectic past.

The closing chorale resounded in my ears, and I almost sang along with Candide and the cast,

You've been a fool, and so have I,
But come and be my wife,
And let us try before we die,
To make a sense of life.
We're neither pure, nor wise, nor good;
We'll do the best we know.
We'll build our house and chop our wood,
And make our garden grow.

Rattling around in our big Victorian house in San Francisco those following weeks, I took an objective view of our Golden Hind adventure. The Ford Foundation brought me a larger view of the theater as a consequence of their bounty. I had always regarded the Company of the Golden Hind as an intensely personal project, too personal as it turned out. Finally I came to ask myself some hard questions. I could see, all too clearly, that I was not a little late in confronting them. I saw that the company needed a full time business and development director, someone who could recruit a responsible board of directors, individuals willing and able to take some responsibility for our annual budget, with connections in the community to increase our public support. Business and development had, of necessity, been one of my strong suits, and I could see myself very effective in that job. But that would mean someone else had to direct the plays. I wasn't prepared for that. I wasn't sure where I could find another Golden Hind director, and realized I had not made any effort to train anyone for the job. Anyhow, I did not want to let go of the company's artistic direction and the soul satisfying challenge the work had been for me.

On the other hand, where would I find a competent business and development director, skilled in fund raising and P.R. and administration, and the salary for some one sufficiently competent and experienced? That would be the only way I could go on as artistic director. I didn't dare to think where I would find someone to replace Suzanna.

I found myself in a labyrinth, with no way out that I could see. It seemed impossible to proceed. I had lost my way, my sense of direction. I was stuck.

I kept the theaters going for a while after "Candide" closed at the end of the planned run. I staged a lack-luster production I'd rather forget, of Brecht's "Goodwoman of Setzuan".

After a few weeks of anguish and panic, I closed the doors of both theaters for good. Declaring bankruptcy with the generous pro bono assistance of an attorney friend, we found the total indebtedness to be about $24,000,. Including several months rent and outstanding invoices payable to the corporate utility companies who hardly took note. I called on some of our regular vendors, like Truitt and White Lumber, and the fabric shop, paint store, and others where we bought our supplies, with my apologies. Without exception, each business owner greeted me with a warm handshake and expression of sympathy for our situation and loss. They each said in their own way that our evenings of wonder and delight would stay with them forever. Just as they have stayed with me.

It was the end for the Company of the Golden Hind.

After-Word

The closing down of the Company of the Golden Hind was duly announced in the local papers. It was almost Christmas and there would be no annual "Knight of the Burning Pestle" as in years gone by. I had been continuing teaching at U.C. so I planned a real get-away vacation. The week before the vacation I ran into Julian Bartlett, Dean of Grace Episcopal Cathedral in San Francisco.

"Rachmael." he said as he took both my hands in his. "I know how much this loss of the Golden Hind must mean to you. It means a lot to us too. We all remember the fine "Murder in the Cathedral" you brought to our church. So tell me, what are your plans, now?"

"Julian," I said, "my only plan right now is to use the coming Christmas vacation to drive down with my skis to Santa Fe and Taos in New Mexico and ski until I drop."

The Dean responded immediately, "I've just returned from the Festival of the Arts at Coventry, England, in their newly renovated cathedral. I wonder if we couldn't have some theater at Grace? Will you promise to call me when you get back from New Mexico and talk to me about that idea?"

Indeed, I promised, and called as we agreed. Our conversation was fruitful and gave rise to the creation of the Cathedral Civic Theater at Grace Cathedral atop Nob Hill in San Francisco. The account of that venture must await another memoir.

As time passes, my memories of our Golden Hind years remain as vivid as ever. It's almost an annual occurrence for me to meet some stranger from our Golden Hind past, someone who had been in the audience, who guards his own memory of some production that came especially close to his heart at the Bella Pacific or the Playbox.

After the first season at the Cathedral, I treated myself to a summer vacation in Mexico. One Saturday in Mexico City, I visited the *Mercado de Sabado*, the Saturday Arts and Crafts Market held in Mexico City's San Angel district. As I was squeezing through the streets and alleyways filled with artisan pottery, hand-woven cloth, turquoise and silver jewelry, a perfect stranger stopped me in my tracks. For a moment I feared I was being accosted by a gentleman I should have been able to recognize but couldn't.

"Excuse me, but aren't you Rachmael ben-Avram from San Francisco?" he asked.

"Yes, I am." I said, a little surprised to be found out in a Mexico City crowd. I wondered if I were guilty of some long forgotten sin. But he was smiling.

"You don't know me," he said. "We've never met. But I know you, Mr. ben-Avram and your Golden Hind. You know you've ruined me forever for Mozart's 'Cosi' with your 'Cosi'." He kept smiling.

"You see," he went on, "I saw your production of "Cosi" in your small theater. It's my favorite Mozart I've seen it many times. Yours was sublime; the best I've ever seen. It made a lasting impression, so I never want to see it staged again. I don't want anything to touch my memory of your lovely production. You see what I mean, when I say you've ruined Mozart's "Cosi" for me?"

I thanked him as he shook my hand heartily. We've never met since then. But his greeting is an ever present comfort in my memory.

I'll add just one more memorable event that heartens me in believing that our Golden Hind vision continues to have a life of its own.

A few years after the Cathedral Civic Theater had begun to make its mark at Grace Cathedral, I received a note from Peter McDonald, the husband of one of our former Golden Hind actresses. Peter sent me a clipping from the monthly British music magazine **The Gramaphone**. It was a review of the LP recording of a new German opera based on "King Lear", by Alibert Reimann. The music critic declared he would limit his review to comments on the music, which he admired. He was enthusiastic about both the music and the libretto which he judged to be a very effective adaptation of Shakespeare's tragedy.

However, he said in closing, he did not wish to see the opera in performance, much as he liked the music. He had been in Berkeley some years previous and had seen a young theater group with the unusual name, The

Company of the Golden Hind. (I've lost the clipping, but I recall the gist of his comment). He wrote that he saw the company's production "on a postage stamp of a stage" in a small commercial laundry space, and found the spirit of the play so completely realized, he could not imagine he would ever see another production equal to it. He vowed he would never even try to see another "Lear" after seeing the young and gifted actors in San Francisco.

To which I say, addressing all who may still be keeping our Golden Hind safe in their memory, please know that it was our intentions and your imagination that made it possible to realize our vision. In Shakespeare's own words,

"We are such stuff as dreams are made on ..."

and ....

"Our revels now are ended."

COMPANY OF THE GOLDEN HIND

Repertoire

Anouilh	The Lark
	Ring Round the Moon (trans.-Christopher Fry).
	Thieves' Carnival
Ansky	The Dybbuk
Beaumont	Knight of the Burning Pestle
Bolt	Man For All Seasons
Brecht	Goodwoman of Setzuan
Chapman/Coxe	Billy Budd
Chayefsky	The Tenth Man
Chekhov	Ivanov
Coward	Blithe Spirit
Eliot	Cocktail Party
	Murder in the Cathedral
Fry	The Lady's Not For Burning
Giraudoux	The Madwoman of Chaillot
Goldsmith	She Stoops to Conquer
Jonson	Volpone
Miller	A View from the Bridge
Milton	Samson Agonistes

Moliere	Imaginary Invalid
	School for Wives
Mowatt	Fashion
O'Casey	Red Roses for Me
O'Neill	Long Day's Journey Into Night
Pirandello	Six Characters in Search of an Author
Shakespeare	Comedy of Errors
	Richard II
	Hamlet
	Romeo and Juliet
	King Lear
	Taming of the Shrew
	Measure for Measure
	The Tempest
Shaw	Arms and the Man
	Candida
	Man and Superman
	Don Juan in Hell
	St. Joan
Ustinov	Love of Four Colonels
Webster	Duchess of Malfi
Wilde	Importance of Being Earnest
Wilder	The Matchmaker
	Our Town
	Skin of Our Teeth
Williams	Glass Menagerie
	Summer and Smoke
	The Wakefield Mystery Plays
	Second Shepherds' Play

, ɔ PERFORMANCES I WAS A PART OF!

Opera

Mozart	Abduction for the Seraglio
	Cosi fan Tutte
	Marriage of Figaro
Paisiello	Barber of Seville
Menotti	Old Maid and the Thief
Baksa	Arai da Capo

Musicals

Arlen	House of Flowers
Bernstein	Candide
	Wonderful Town
Rodgers/Hart	Boys from Syracuse
Wilson	The Boy Friend

FANNY

KERR/ANDERSON   GOLDILOCKS

CATHEDRAL   CIVIC PLAYERS

CRUCIBLE
SAINT JOAN
TARTUFFE

LOCAL PBS
WINDOW OF THE GLEN
MAN AND SUPERMAN
IMPORTANCE OF BEING EARNEST

Made in the USA
Columbia, SC
03 July 2017